MW01288689

Benched: What I Gained When I Lost It All

"Benched by Rebecca Fussell is a poignant account of losing everything to gain it all. She paints a beautiful word picture of how, when everything, every dream we've held dear, disappears, God alone remains. And not only does He remain, but He also encourages us, cheers for us, carries us, loves us, sits beside us and holds us in our seasons of devastation. It's a story of life birthed from death, peace from turmoil, faithfulness from betrayal, and of the steadfast love of the Father in all seasons of our lives. *Benched* is a beautiful romance—the story of a faithful Father pursuing the heart of His beloved.

> — CAROL JAMES, author of *Rescuing Faith,*
> *The Waiting, Mary's Christmas Surprise,* and
> *Season of Hope* (coming in 2020)

"Take a seat next to Rebecca as she courageously shares her heartbreaking tale. Brilliant writing and bold expression consistently intersect her story with the lessons God provided. A treasure-trove of wise counsel for the one seated and lost. It is a beneficial resource for those watching from the sidelines as friends are shockingly and suddenly benched. Adamant yet pliable, steadfast yet cautious, she tells of deep disappointment and devastation attempting to sway her off the bench, but Rebecca vulnerably reveals how an abiding faith in Jesus kept her seated and steadfastly trusting in God's plan for her future."

> — ELLEN HARBIN, speaker, Bible study teacher,
> author of the *STAND Bible Study series*, and
> founder of the STAND Women's Conference

"'Put me in, Coach, I'm ready to play!'[1] is the cry of every athlete. Being benched is every athlete's fear. Rebecca Fussell captures this benched feeling in her beautifully crafted memoir. She invites you into her hurts and disappointments and then into the rescue that Jesus provides. Her story is encouraging and honest and illustrates the steadfast faithfulness of God."

> — JEANNE HEWITT, author of *Metamorphosis of*
> *the Mind*

"Reading *Benched* is like sitting down with a friend over a cup of coffee. As Rebecca shares her personal story of growth through loss, the tears, the humor and the hope will all encourage you whatever storm you're facing."

> — DALYN WOODS, blogger and author of *My*
> *Sister's Keeper, Exposed* and *The Bride Escape*
> (coming 2020)

"*Benched* by Rebecca Fussell is in some ways a hard book to read as you experience her trauma. Rebecca has woven pain and humor together to address what God is up to when bad things happen to good people. Through the journey of divorce and recovery, Rebecca has opened her heart to share the gut-level pain and struggles that accompany a deep loss. She has done it in a way that has you crying and laughing at the same time. This book is a taste of Southern charm in the midst of trauma as she weaves word pictures and concepts into spiritual truths that are timeless. What you read in her book is what you get in person with Rebecca; a genuine and authentic experience of God walking you through the deep places of life."

— SCOTT BRITTIN, president of Grace Ministries International

"Life rarely pans out as planned. Storms come. Hurt and heartache are real. In *Benched*, Rebecca Fussell takes the reader on a captivating and transparent journey of her own story as she shares what she gained when she lost it all. When life hurts, we wrestle to believe what we know to be true. We doubt. We fear. We question. *Benched* helps readers find to Whom, how and where to find hope when they feel all hope is gone as they discover (or maybe rediscover) that God is really real in real life. I highly recommend it!"

— STEPHANIE SHOTT, Bible teacher, author of *The Making of a Mom* and founder of The MOM Initiative

"In *Benched*, Rebecca Fussell offers us the opportunity to walk with her through heartache and growth. When she realizes how dramatically her marriage is going off the rails, she turns to God in a panic. *This wasn't supposed to happen!* But through the turmoil of a crumbling marriage, she comes to new understandings about God and her place nestled securely in His hands. This book is filled with quirky, relatable humor, open-hearted tenderness, and simple principles for cultivating a life that overflows with joy and gratitude."

— JOSEPH MAZERAC, author of *Into the Attic of the World* and host of the Blue Deck Podcast

Benched

Benched

What I Gained When I Lost It All

Rebecca Lynn Fussell

Benched: What I Gained When I Lost It All
Copyright © 2019 Rebecca Fussell
WITH ALL YOUR ART PUBLISHING, Jacksonville, FL
ISBN: 9781689025133

All rights reserved. No portion of this book may be reproduced, stored in a retrieval system, or transmitted in any form or by any means except for brief quotations in critical reviews or articles.

Unless otherwise indicated, Scripture is taken from the KING JAMES VERSION (KJV): KING JAMES VERSION, public domain.

Scriptures quotations marked NIV are taken from THE HOLY BIBLE, NEW INTERNATIONAL VERSION®, NIV® Copyright © 1973, 1978, 1984, 2011 by Biblica, Inc.™ Used by permission. All rights reserved worldwide.

Scripture quotations marked ESV are from the ESV® Bible (The Holy Bible, English Standard Version®), copyright © 2001 by Crossway, a publishing ministry of Good News Publishers. Used by permission. All rights reserved."

The stories in this book are true. In some instances the names of people and places have been changed for the privacy of the individuals involved. Events and conversations have been constructed from the author's best recollection.

Cover photo: Hal Ozart @ Unsplashed

Cover Design: Joseph Mazerac

FOR MY MOTHER

The one who taught me to pray,
Who lives the motto, "Where there's a will, there's a way,"
Who loves fiercely and sacrifices deeply,
And who, when I was a little girl, could make all my stuffed
animals come alive during story time.

TABLE OF CONTENTS

A NOTE FROM THE AUTHOR

The people and events in this book are real, and
I have described them from my best recollection.
In some instances, the names of people and
places have been changed to protect the
privacy of those involved.

INTRODUCTION

I don't suppose anyone expects to get divorced, *especially* not good Christian girls.

I know I sure didn't. After all, isn't a lifelong marriage one of the perks of obedience?

My younger self thought that following God's plan would ensure that your life would not be affected by the crippling "D" word. I loved God, only dated Christian guys and kept myself unspotted from the world. I read my Bible and prayed. I even fasted regularly to guarantee that God would spare me the heartache and humiliation of marrying the wrong mate.

Imagine my dismay when I walked out of the Fulton County Court House with the new official title of "divorcée." Even after months of the process and waiting for my husband (now legally my ex-husband) to come to his senses, I *still* couldn't believe he didn't want me anymore.

But more debilitating than the suffocating pain of his rejection, this certificate provided living proof that everything I had believed, everything I had done to safeguard this from happening, had failed. I had lost it all – my home, my husband and best friend, my identity, my value as a wife, my financial security, my friends, my hope of motherhood, but most unbearable of all, my understanding of a God I had trusted to guard and protect my heart.

I'd been benched.

You may find yourself in a similar state. One minute you're enjoying a refreshing afternoon, sipping lemonade on the front porch. With the blink of an eye or perhaps something you'd seen brewing in the distance, a catastrophic storm cloud has swept through your being, leaving you ravaged and stunned with the aftermath. Life-as-you-know-it has changed forever, despite your best efforts to keep everything in its place. It is in part for you that I write these words.

I realize that these are my experiences, but they are filled with life-changing principles anyone can use if you are willing. I want you to know that although the pain you feel cannot be exonerated by words, I pray these thoughts will encourage you. May they guide you like a map down the passageway toward treasures only found in the depths of that pain. May you, like me, find that what I thought I had, what I thought I knew, I now see as imitation compared to *what I gained when I lost it all.*

This book is not intended to tell my story as if somehow

my circumstances were more devastating or more noteworthy than anyone else's heartache. No doubt there are countless people with more tragic details surrounding the loss in their lives. Rather, the aim of this book is first and foremost to celebrate the healing power of a magnificent God who desires to make Himself known to those who will seek Him; a God who gives hope when all is lost; and a God who risks our misunderstanding so His love can seep into the deepest crevasses of our lives to make us abundant and full.

This book is also a testament to the beautiful body of Christ and the people God used to breathe life back into my soul. Not until Heaven will they comprehend how vital they were to my healing. They don't know it yet, but their investment into my life has had eternal impact on the kingdom of God. For when one of us struggles, all are affected. When one of us is made whole, the entire Kingdom benefits. Only time will tell how far-reaching the ripple effect of their kindness and love has extended, and how many lives it has improved. May those of you reading this book be inspired by the example of the sacrificial and God-fearing people He put into my life, people willing to get involved, to roll up their sleeves and love when life is messy.

Life does not come in neat, happy packages. It's often scarred and bruised. Ultimately this book is for the nearly 45% of married people who find themselves left with broken dreams, a trash bag of doubt and a boatload of scary vulnerabilities in their future.[1] This book is a candid look at the life-altering realities that all too often even good

Christian people want to sweep under the rug. Too many believers have not and will not reach their fullest potential because they refuse to take an honest look at the pain and questions, thereby spending the rest of their lives with an open sore oozing on every part of their existence. Many have fallen for the old adage that time heals all wounds believing that if they just ignore the issue long enough, eventually it will disappear into oblivion, and everyone will live happily ever after. Unfortunately, that statement misguides many into a life of masquerade. Relationships remain shallow because, even years after the event, deep down in the pit of the soul exist haunting questions and wounds still as fresh as the day they received the first blow. Without true healing, they remain vulnerable and unable to move past the stage of denial or grief or apathy. They wonder why they continue in a cycle of bad choices.

But there is another route to take. Follow me on my own journey of healing and growth. Learn from my shortcomings and temptations. Let my experience of being benched next to God's mercy and grace encourage you to embrace this season of your life, knowing you have a God who loves you too much to leave you alone. In the end, may you rejoice in sharing what you gained when you lost it all.

PROLOGUE

The ground beneath my feet had been eroding undetected for years.

Undetected? Okay sure, there were a few glitches along the way, but everything was fine now. I believed that. Really, I did. However, on this particular day, my life crumbled faster than a dry piece of cornbread.

The day promised nothing out of the ordinary, just middle of the workweek routine.

Well, except that my husband and I would need to switch cars.

Typically, JP let me drive the Camry. It actually had functioning air conditioning *and* heat, it rarely ever died at the stoplight, and it was just overall prettier than our second car, which we nicknamed "Old Blue." He had to attend a funeral that morning, and we both agreed it would be disrespectful for him to hold up the entire funeral processional going from car to car asking if anyone could give the old girl a jump.

Switching vehicles seemed like such an unremarkable detail.

It turned out to be one of the most significant things that has ever happened to me.

Attending the funeral that morning allowed JP to sport a sharp suit and tie for a change. His handsome, athletic build set off the sparkle in his crystal blue eyes. I doted while straightening his tie. "Hey mister, you clean up nice." A look of contentment instantly spit-shined his whole being. I could feel that we were thinking the same thing in that moment: oh, how we looked forward to the day when he would be much more than a teaching assistant!

While I taught first grade at a little private school, JP worked as a paraprofessional at Wilson High School, right around the corner from our tiny rental home. Being on staff there allowed him to coach basketball. Although his job ranked lowest on the pay scale, and coaching didn't pay any extra, we hoped it would prove to be a critical career step toward his dream of coaching a college team. He just needed a way to break into that arena, and Wilson High seemed like a perfect opportunity. The varsity boy's coach—we called him Coach—happened to be a former head coach at a state university. It was common knowledge that this man's caliber of coaching ensured that one day he'd return to the collegiate level. And when he did, maybe, just maybe he'd take JP (and me) with him.

In spite of the huge financial sacrifice, I supported the decision. I believed in my husband and knew he'd be an excellent head coach one day.

After class that afternoon, I pulled Old Blue into the high school parking lot to switch cars so I could have air conditioning to run my errands. I spotted where JP had left the Camry and parked in the empty space beside it. The next logical step would've been to open the car door and get out. But my eye caught the sight of JP's satchel nestled between Old Blue's worn seats and the console.

On a whim, I decided to look inside it.

I don't know why I looked.

But maybe once a trust has been broken—no matter if the offense was slight, no matter how many times the earth has circled around the sun since the latest breach of confidence, no matter if there have been apologies said and forgiveness given—I don't guess it's ever fully restored.

I had no *immediate* reason to be suspicious.

In fact, a couple weeks prior JP and I had a great heart-to-heart talk. I unleashed all my pent-up emotions and explained, "I feel like the school and Coach take advantage of your time. If they didn't give you so many duties, then maybe you could find another part-time job to help us with our long-term goals."

He'd assured me, "Beck, I know. But I believe it'll pay off someday. Coach may be part of the big break I need. I want him to see how hard I'm willing to work."

If only it could have been that simple.

In reality, my frustration started way before his current job at Wilson High School. We'd been waiting eight years for his "big break," a season of life I wanted to embrace whole-heartedly.

Deep down, a nagging question kept surfacing: I wondered if *I* mattered to him. The idea of "us" never made it to the forefront. In our almost eight years of marriage, we had lived in four different homes in two states, and at the start of every school year, our lives had been uprooted to chase another coaching opportunity. This time it landed us in Atlanta.

To add to the frustration, during this time I wasn't able to conceive, which caused heartache too tender to touch. We'd exhausted every medical treatment that insurance would cover with nothing but scars and tears to show for it. The next step in our dream of parenting would cost us money—a lot of money. But it was worth it to me, and JP had given me the impression he wanted children too.

The day in the doctor's office a year earlier had confirmed it.

All the air escaped from the room as the doctor explained my surgery had been unsuccessful. Additional steps would be required. At least I think that's what he said. Finally, JP asked the question I feared to voice but felt frantic to know. "Are you telling me, she can still have a baby?" His voice sounded shaky and thin, yet somehow tenacious and firm.

The doctor assured him, "There are excellent possibilities. And yes, she could still have a baby."

My lungs exhaled a deep sigh of relief as JP's body slumped back into the chair.

Leaving the office that day, my husband seemed committed to prioritizing our funds. We'd have to save up for the procedure, but we were on the same page.

The fact that my husband shared in my grief cradled my wounded heart. His gentleness was like a white-gloved curator caring for a fragile artifact. He desired our union to bring life into this world. Nothing could be more intimate or holy in my eyes. Although we didn't have a lot of money, no one would love and enjoy their baby more than we would. I rested in believing God would use this heartache to strengthen our faith and love.

⁕

But ever since that day in the doctor's office, I'd been confused. Neither of those things—baby or permanent roots—appeared anywhere near the horizon. I needed to know if JP's hopes had changed or at what point *we* would ever become a priority.

On one hand, I wanted to be okay with the current plan. I believed in him. The last thing I wanted to do was to discourage him from his dream.

On the other hand, I wanted to shout, "Grow up and provide for us!" That felt selfish and petty. Wives were supposed to be their husband's number one fan, right? But then why did my heart tell me something was wrong with this picture?

One day I couldn't swallow it any longer. My frustration fueled my courage.

"Can we talk for a minute?" My tone strained.

He stopped, looked at me with a guarded expression, and then sat stiff-backed on the couch. A blind man would have seen his reluctance. Men hate that question. I should have started differently, but at least he was sitting.

I took a deep breath and prayed that he'd hear the ache in my heart without interpreting it as complaining or sounding like I didn't believe in him. "You know I love you, right?"

His brow furrowed as he nodded.

"And you know how much I believe in you as a coach and *love* watching your teams play, right?" I felt like I was walking through a minefield.

He shrugged. "Yeah, I know."

"It's just . . . Well, I want you to succeed. I do. With all my heart, I do. And I support you. But sometimes I, um . . . I wonder if I mean as much to you as your coaching does?"

I had finally spit it out. I felt like such a baby asking, but I needed to hear it from him.

He let out a chuckle and smiled. "Yes, Rebecca. I love coaching, but you mean more to me." His lighthearted tone urged me forward to bolder questions and thoughts I'd been harboring. He listened with that *"You silly girl, that's what I love about you"* look on his face.

As the conversation ended, he leaned in close and planted a tender kiss on my forehead: his playful affection kissing away a mound of burden. I had expressed my frustration and he seemed to receive my words as I meant them. What a relief.

In return, he had convinced me how much he cared about our future . . . and about me.

So that's not why I looked in the briefcase.

1

POWERLESS . . . NOT!

To this day, I don't know what possessed me to look in my husband's briefcase, but I did. I found the typical things you'd expect in a coach's satchel: his playbook, a few random diagrams of offensive plays, his portfolio, a yellow legal pad. I noticed the side zipper was open, so I ran my hand inside the pocket and pulled out its contents.

Now that was strange. What is this? *Who is . . .?*

In my hands, I rotated two pictures of a slightly overweight young woman posing in a bikini at the beach— or somewhere. I had never seen her before. I guessed her age to be a few years younger than me.

She wore a bright smile conveying that she relished every minute of the photographer's attention. I stared in bewilderment trying to fill in the blank spaces now bombarding my thoughts like hail stones.

I froze. Questions lined up in my head faster than thirsty kindergartners after recess, scrambling to be first at the water fountain. *Who is this woman? Does JP know her? Obviously, he knows her. Why else would he have these pictures? She does have a pretty smile and looks like she's a lot of fun. Is this what I think it is? But he just told me a few weeks ago...*

My heart raced and jerked. I determined not to panic. I needed time to think. I drove home and began to mull over the events of the last hour. I came to a simple conclusion. I just needed to ask him about it. The whole thing probably amounted to nothing. Even if it were something, surely JP would say, "Rebecca, that was a stupid temptation. I started to fall for it, but I realized it was crazy." He'd blush and say, "I forgot they were even in there."

After crafting my opening statement, I decided to page JP.

Yes. Page—as in an old-fashioned beeper. In the late 90's, before everyone and their ten-year-old had a cell phone, our meager budget didn't allow such a luxury, so I paged him 911. Paging each other 911 indicated an emergency, and we knew to call immediately. So I paged, anticipating his quick response.

Nothing.

I paged again—911. Still nothing. I waited, bravely at first. But as the clock ticked, the silence seemed to confirm my worst fear.

He had never gone this long without calling me back. The panic of what could be started to overtake my senses. My legs felt weak, but I couldn't stop pacing.

He was ignoring me. I could've been in a wreck or deathly ill. *Why is he not answering? Does he know that I know about the pictures?*

Eventually my fear morphed into a consuming anger. He had practice tonight, but he should have been home long ago. The questions pinged off the walls. *Where is he? Why hasn't he called me? I could be in serious trouble. Oh, this cannot be happening. He wouldn't do this to me. I'm sure of it . . . No, I'm not sure.*

Several hours had passed since I'd discovered the pictures. As the chill of night replaced the afternoon sun, my anger transformed into a desperate frazzle. Pacing my small house, too nervous to sit, it started coming together. All the late nights, the sudden lack of finances, the emotional distance: it had all been so recent and out of character for him, I'd only just begun to notice. We'd always done things together, but lately, his usual invitations for me to join him had been replaced with more vague information regarding his schedule.

He seemed uninterested in our diminishing finances, working a silly part-time job, volunteering all his time to the team. He had no problem with me working two jobs to keep us afloat, while he bought new clothes and shoes. I'm all for looking nice, but not when we are struggling to pay the rent.

I decided I needed to find him, and I needed to find him now.

It's funny how life works. Apparently, our marriage had been hanging on by a thread, yet I had been resting in it as if I were lounging in a comfy tree hammock. It was as though I was floating peacefully several feet in the air, and in an instant, the rope snapped, and I found myself falling headfirst into the river beneath me, a river I didn't even realize existed. The shock of the cold, icy water muted my cries for help and sent me sputtering and splashing downstream as the current swept me away from everything familiar and lovely.

I begged God to help me find JP. I couldn't take one more second of idle waiting. My hunt ended in a successful capture and I found him scouting a game across town, laughing and shooting the breeze with some buddies. Even though I had physically located him, I had no earthly idea what had happened to my darling husband. His body was there, but all the love and companionship I thought we possessed had somehow disintegrated into the night air. In its place JP emanated a smug apathy that barely tolerated my presence.

The noise of the crowded gym faded away as I sat in the bleachers next to him. Trying to hold my frenzy at bay, I struggled to keep my voice calm. "Why didn't you answer my page?"

"We'll talk about it when I get home."

My jaw clenched. "No, we'll talk about it now.

He turned toward his buddies. "I'm busy now. We'll talk about it later."

Normally my will took a backseat to his suggestions. Not this time. My lips barely opened as I spoke. "No. You *better* come with me now, or I won't be home when you get there." I hadn't planned on saying that, but the minute I heard it come out of my mouth, I knew I meant it.

After a longer pause than I expected, he sauntered out of

his seat, and amid high fives and fist bumps apologized to all his pals for leaving early. Then he followed several paces behind my determined self out the gymnasium door and into the parking lot.

"Hand me the keys. I'll drive," he said.

JP always drove when we were together.

"No." *Where did that come from?* "I'm driving." I couldn't believe the words spewing out of my mouth. I rarely told JP what to do, but I did that night. I headed toward the driver's door.

JP stopped, unsure how to interpret my newfound boldness. Like a scolded child who knew when to cut his losses, he slid into the passenger's side. As soon as the door shut, he employed a new strategy. He began to snicker.

His carefree attitude sent me—already an emotional basket case—into a furious tailspin I didn't know how to stop. Nothing I said or did could make him care.

Never before had I felt so wild or helpless. I shouldn't have gotten behind the wheel that night, but there I was flying down the road, swerving between cars and taking corners at almost full speed.

He kept repeating, "Calm down! Watch where you're going."

My driving was out of control, but I didn't care. The angrier I got the more he smirked.

Once we made it home, I don't remember much about confronting JP about the pictures, except that the lady also worked at his school.

"She gave me the pictures." And he added for emphasis,

"Because I asked her for them."

That part he made clear. *She hadn't initiated anything. He had pursued her.*

A dagger pierced my heart and my whole body went weak. I couldn't believe this morning began as a regular day with a kiss goodbye and "See ya tonight."

Soon my anger wore down into suffocating despair. My incoherent thoughts swirled. I didn't know the details of JP's new interest, but I sensed us heading toward destruction.

"We can't live like this. We need help," I said.

For the first time all evening, he revealed a tinge of softness. "I agree."

That night, he voluntarily slept in our spare room. I never suggested it; he just did. Perhaps he thought that's what he ought to do, or maybe he meant to underscore the point that *"Yes, I'm interested in this woman and I don't have any regrets about it."* I didn't know.

Up to that point in my life, I had no real reference for the pain Christ endured for us on the cross. Although I didn't claim to understand the depth of His grief, after that night I absolutely understood how someone could die of a broken heart. The intensity of the word "agony" became rich with meaning as I suffered the most dread-filled, hopeless night of my life. I didn't know a person's hurt could pierce that deep.

Looking back at Christ's willingness to bear such anguish on my behalf, I'm overwhelmed by His unrelenting pursuit of me despite the cost. But in that moment, no verse I had ever heard or memorized even made sense to me. My shallow prayers sputtered nothing more than, *"Oh, God it hurts! Oh, God . . . Please. Help me!"* Over and over, I cried and pleaded.

I didn't sleep a wink. I tried listening to music. I tried moving to the living room. To the outside steps. Back to my bedroom. I felt like a caged animal about to lose my mind, all the while hearing the gentle snores of my beloved in the next room.

What is it about another person's oblivion toward your pain that stings so deeply? JP's quiet, untroubled rest spit into my gaping wound. All that I had believed about our marriage and life *and God* I no longer recognized, and it scared the breath out of me. JP's peace enlarged the situation like a magnifying glass: "The man I love more than any other person in the world does not care if I live or die. I am the only one hurting tonight." The pit in the center of my soul pointed me toward my worst fear.

Life as I had known it would never be the same again.

I wondered if daylight would ever come. I had no idea what I'd do when it showed up, but until then, the darkness smothered me. JP and I had agreed we'd talk more in the morning. To me, that meant we both needed to call our jobs, tell them we would not be coming in today and seek guidance immediately. In my opinion, we had a crisis on our hands. Our marriage was dangling over a cliff. We needed help. Now.

Morning came, and JP agreed that we needed counsel, but he wasn't so keen on the now part. He had no intention of missing work. My mind darted—like being at the scene of an accident before help arrives. I didn't have a clue where to turn for help.

While JP showered for work, I took a big risk. I decided to call my principal and hint to her that I needed help. Perhaps she could guide me toward what to do. My heart pounded as her phone rang. She answered. Half whispering so JP couldn't hear me and half trying to keep my voice from cracking, I mustered up something like, "Maryellen, it's Rebecca. I'm sorry, but I'm not going to be able to make it in today. I can't go into the details, but I have a serious emergency."

Whether my faltering voice gave it away or just her usual sixth sense, her gentle voice asked, "Does any of this have to do with JP?"

My heart skipped in relief. "It does. And I absolutely don't know what to do." My bravery dissipated as my voice whimpered out the last line.

She gave me the name of a counselor of hers and told me to call him around 9:00 a.m. "Be sure to tell him that I gave you his number."

Just talking to her on the phone and discussing an action plan calmed me through JP's morning routine. Even though I didn't tell her the nature of my tragedy, sharing a bit of my desperation gave a little strength to my waning composure. Composure I lacked. My acting like a full-fledged maniac the night before had only escalated the situation, and JP had reciprocated by making fun of me. I didn't want to experience a repeat of that this morning, and having a plan helped.

❧

Part of my anger and frustration came from a sense of helplessness. When an event I didn't choose or expect hurled my life into chaos, I needed to remember that I wasn't completely powerless. I still had the decision-making authority over how I would respond.

I decided to call the counselor. I also decided not to allow myself to react by engaging in a screaming match. I may not have been able to influence my beloved, but I could decide on a plan of action regarding the events forced upon me.

I *did* have choices. Regardless of how elementary it seemed at the moment, taking these small steps forward steadied my mind and calmed my heart.

❧

WHAT I GAINED: When life unraveled before my eyes, focusing on something I could control reminded me I wasn't powerless. I could decide on a plan of action. No matter how simple the plan, it helped.

2

PRETEND, BUT FOR REAL

I wondered if the world had stopped spinning and if nine a.m. would ever come. Finally, the clock struck, and it was time to call the number Maryellen had offered me.

On the other end of the line, the receptionist said that the counselor was unavailable, but she would give him my message.

I sure hoped so, but I pictured my plea for help being mysteriously swallowed up by a phone message black hole. My insides felt like a stick shift that couldn't find the gear at the red light.

Maryellen must have called and encouraged the counselor, Scott, to return my call as soon as possible. Within a few minutes he called me back. Thank God for good friends.

I felt foolish as I tried to articulate the depth of my pain over the phone to a man I'd never met. Words sounded so trivial. How could he possibly understand how deeply I loved my husband, the sacrifices I'd made and how desperately I'd tried to be a good wife? I imagined all the thoughts going through his head like, *"Oh boy, here we go again"* or, *"I wonder what the real story is."* But at the moment, my desperation and fear trumped my awkwardness and pride. I needed help.

I rattled off as much as I dared. I knew his schedule was full and that he'd called as a favor to our mutual friend. However, Scott listened to my scatterbrained half-sentences and broken thoughts. Although he didn't know me, his kind responses validated my pain and acknowledged the seriousness of the situation.

Then he asked, "Are you willing to try something?"

At this point I would have braved walking a tightrope across Niagara Falls if I thought it would help. "Yes, I'll try anything. Please, tell me."

"Imagine yourself writing JP's name on a scrap of paper. Then picture it tucked into the palm of your hand. Can you do that?"

I half-chuckled. He obviously didn't know *pretend* is my middle name. "Yes, absolutely I've got a great imagination."

"Okay next, visualize yourself opening up your hand. Can you do that?"

"Yes." My voice was soft, but confident.

"Then picture God taking the paper from you. You'll need to trust Him to hold onto it for you and do with it as He sees best." He paused and added, "Then do the same thing with your marriage."

His words resonated, and an unexpected peace swept over me. I told him I would certainly try it. I hung up the phone and dropped to my knees beside my overstuffed chair.

I pictured the scene just as he said. First, JP's name. I imagined his name on a scrap of paper. Easy enough. But as it came time to envision opening my hand, my fingers locked into place, afraid to expose the name I adored.

The physical struggle to open my hand shocked me. I hadn't expected to experience the literal ache in my fingers during an *imaginary* exercise. It reminded me of times I'd held onto something for too long and needed my other hand to pry open my fingers in order to release the object. But open I did.

With my palm exposed, I resisted the next step of allowing God's hand to remove the paper. Tears flowed as freely as my questions, *"But God, don't you know I've given JP everything that's precious and sacred to me. He knows me in ways I've never allowed another man to know me. What will happen to him? God, please don't give up on him. You are going to give him back to me, right?"*

No answer.

"You're silent, God. What does that mean? But I thought You would . . ."

I stopped.

Expectations are a funny thing. Somehow in my twisted, controlling mind I figured that even though I'd released the scrap of paper, God would still let me *see* it. Silly me. I imagined I'd have input, or at least receive updates on how things moved along.

Instead, the exercise played out more like the release of a

helium balloon slipping away from me and floating out of sight. It appeared the most careless act a person could commit—letting go of the one you love into the ginormous sky overhead. Yet somehow, beyond what I could see, I needed to trust that God had a hold of that string.

I hoped the Lord would answer my questions, but He sent me a picture instead. I envisioned myself a speck on the earth suspended in the massive universe. In that scenario, my questions peeped in comparison to the wisdom and vastness of the Creator God, and I knew I had a choice. I could trust Him in faith or hold on to my solutions and panic.

Last night, the hold-on-and-panic method could've landed me on the "Crazy Woman of the Year" list. Entrusting JP over to a God who promised that His thoughts were higher than my thoughts and His ways higher than mine proved the only sensible option.

I hoped to catch a glimpse of where God put the paper. But I could picture Him with raised eyebrows and tilted head saying, "Rebecca . . ."

I let God take it and relinquished my control to Him.

After a deep breath, I repeated the process, writing "my marriage" on the second make-believe scrap. I cried deep sobs and felt the tension in my fingers as my imagination pried them open again.

What if I didn't like how this turned out? Maybe I shouldn't do it. But once again, I was reminded that the hold-on-and-twist-JP's-arm plan had proven a useless strategy. I opened my hand and asked God to take it.

I meant it.

I wanted to release JP and our marriage into His safekeeping.

This moment officially started me on a new, albeit unwanted path. I didn't know it at the time, but in less than twenty-four hours after the initial unraveling of my life, from a counselor I'd never met, I received what had become one of the greatest weapons in my arsenal of faith. To this day, this exercise is a staple of defense the Enemy detests.

Throughout the next several months, every time that panicky feeling swept over me, I'd picture myself knees bent, hands outstretched, releasing those papers to God. My mind would journey back to that morning beside my chair until it became like a well-worn path to a cherished spot in my memory.

I found comfort in this thought from A.W. Tozer: "Everything is safe which we commit to him, and nothing is really safe which is not so committed." I echoed his prayer as my own, *"Father, I want to know Thee, but my cowardly heart fears to give up its toys. I cannot part with them without inward bleeding, and I do not try to hide from Thee the terror of the parting. I come trembling, **but I do come**"*[1] (emphasis mine).

So, I took the first baby steps on the journey of learning what I would gain when I lost it all.

WHAT I GAINED: Although my ability to control my husband and the outcome of our marriage was just an illusion, I still needed to release that imaginary hold. Not for God's sake, but for my own.

3

A HAND IN THE DARK

I could forgive JP. I knew that.

My friends and family on the other hand? They might not be as willing to kiss and make up as I was. And when this escapade blew over—as I knew it would—I couldn't risk a permanent stain splashed over JP's face every time my loved ones thought of him.

No. I'd handle this in private.

In the days that followed, guarding JP's reputation became my main goal, no matter the cost. That objective left me no choice but to do what too many good, respectable Christians do: I kept quiet.

I didn't tell anyone about the pictures or the resulting conversation. I hid the ugly truth behind a closed door, which I only cracked open long enough to shove my shame and fear inside to keep it company. After bolting the door shut, I wiped my sweating palms on my skirt, swiped at my bangs and entered survival mode.

Doing this felt wifely. Brave. Christian.

But in reality, covering up such an awful secret was like holding my breath and trying to act normal at the same time. This charade required much more moxie than I'd bargained for. All I had ever known seemed locked up in a vault and someone had thrown away the key. Some days I couldn't even remember my phone number.

I couldn't go forward. I had no idea what the future held. I couldn't go backward. No matter how I longed to run away or bury myself under the covers I couldn't erase the present.

The severity of my situation squelched my appetite, and the pounds began to fall off, leaving my clothes baggy and my face gaunt. My hair hung limp and the sparkle in my eye dimmed. Each day, the sham eroded a bit further, and my strength to bear up under the weight of my sadness dissipated.

Many days, I fought off the despair like a soldier fighting for his life. It felt like any moment the strength to take the next breath would be gone, and I'd end up in a puddle on the ground. Everyone's mouth would gape open in shock and say, "Oh, my goodness. What's wrong with Rebecca?"

Sure enough, one day my empty house closed in on me.

JP said he'd be home late—said he had to scout a game across town. Whether he told me the truth or not, I didn't know. I longed to believe him, but I feared being played for a fool.

Alone in my quiet abode with only my imagination to

keep me company created a bad environment for my fragile state. I needed to get out of the house. Besides, it was time for JP to come home and wonder where *I* was for a change. *Yeah… maybe that would snap him back into marital focus.*

Right.

I jumped in the car and headed to my favorite discount dress shop. But instead of providing a distraction, my flipping through overcrowded clothes racks somehow fueled the hidden ache inside. I didn't need a new outfit. I *needed* a giant eraser to remove the past month.

As I squeezed between circular frames crammed with dresses, deep down I questioned. *Would erasing the recent events even solve the problem?* Something told me this wounded marriage had been on life support for years. If that was true, how could I have been so naïve?

The shock of this discovery left me feeling like a smiling plastic doll maneuvering through life with a bleeding person on the inside trying to cry out, *"Can't anyone see I'm dying in here? Please. Someone, help me!"* But no one heard me. All people could see were the painted blue eyes and fixed pink lips on the doll's face.

Hearing the other shoppers and cashiers laughing and chatting meaningless gibberish infuriated me. Could they not see the seriousness of life? Did they not recognize that people all around them were in deep anguish?

Apparently not.

Regardless of my inward scolding, they had the audacity to keep joking and enjoying the evening. I hadn't told anyone about my trauma, yet it lit my hair on fire when no one cared. The more they laughed, the more unhinged I became.

I figured it best not to interrupt their shopping pleasure with fits of hysteria about the gravity of life. Staying much longer in that scene could have landed me in a straitjacket for all I knew. I sure didn't want to hang around to see what that looked like.

I fled to my car and drove home with hope of at least part of my plan still intact . . . until I pulled up to a dark house.

He was still not home.

In the midst of this survival mode, my emotional pendulum swung from one extreme to the other and hit every possible feeling in between.

At times, my heart burst brave with gratefulness knowing I belonged to God. I was His daughter. He would not fail me. Somehow we'd come out of this stronger and purified.

As strange as it sounds, brief moments of relief also swept over me. Deep down I'd always suspected that something stood as a roadblock in JP's relationship with God, and consequently, me. Until now, I supposed myself half-crazy or hypersensitive, but the briefcase revelation confirmed my gut intuition. Truth sets people free. Once we sorted through this dirty laundry, we could finally move past *stuck* and get on with God's amazing plan for our lives.

Other times, the pendulum swung way out of whack and apathy ruled. Maybe I didn't want to put forth the herculean effort this relationship required. I was alone all the time anyway. My evenings consisted of busying myself—so as not to go crazy imagining where he was—while waiting for him to come home. Most nights I'd give up and go to bed alone, wondering.

On these days, the million-dollar question swarmed my thoughts: *How could I ever trust him again?*

Occasionally, he showed signs of remorse, if that's what you'd call it. It always centered on *him* and how unhappy or frustrated *he* felt.

He'd come home. Head down. Quiet. Eyes begging me to ask. So of course, I did. "How was your day?"

His head would lift and out it would come. He'd blurt out every negative thing on his mind. Then, he'd want to be near me. Snuggling close on the couch, I could feel his body relax.

At first, it flattered me. *See, he needs me and wants me in his life.* But the subject of my day never seemed to come up. In my heart it felt off. Out of balance. Not the way God designed marriage. I felt more like a mom, not a cherished wife to be cared for.

After the apathy swing, I'd beat myself up for not desiring to fight for my marriage. Then a spark would hit. I'd grit my teeth and re-enter the mental and spiritual battle, remembering that God specialized in restoring the direst of circumstances. A mighty hope would ensue, and I held white-knuckled onto the truth from Jeremiah 32:27, *"Behold,*

I am the Lord, the God of all flesh; is there anything too hard for me?"

God would see us through. I simply needed to hold out a little longer.

JP's recent rejection felt like a bad dream we could put behind us when we woke up. Surely our marriage had just hit a roadblock. I determined to stick with my plan of keeping our problems secret. One day we'd look back on this and agree it was the best thing that ever happened to us.

Surely . . .

But amidst my bravest moments, the pendulum would swing again. Destructive thoughts dropped in my heart like a surprise enemy air attack. *This is not a dream. What if JP wants out of our marriage?* What would I do? How would I survive in this humungous city on my own? My meager teacher's salary barely paid the rent and light bill. I couldn't fathom the solutions, nor did I want to.

The fear blurred my perspective and excluded any account of God in my life. I needed a moment, a time-out to catch my breath. But even when I did consider God, I wondered to what extent He would come through. I'd faced my fair share of heartache and disappointment, but this crisis beat out any I'd experienced in the past. The more I tried to figure it out on my own, the more panic dominated.

While a soul cannot physically be seen or touched, it is as real and pertinent as the wind. And like the wind, the effects of a withered soul show up all over, no matter how hard we try to hide it.

Under normal circumstances, the teachers' weekly prayer meeting boosted my spirits. The privilege of pulling aside for a few minutes with godly colleagues always inspired me.

On this particular day, I sat towards the back of the group, as I had done numerous times, and I listened to the conversation, the announcements for the week and a few prayer requests.

Then without warning, I began to shake.

I didn't notice it at first. My insides had been trembling for days, and periodically this inward quaking escaped into outward shaking. But I had always been able to regain my composure and stuff it back inside.

Not today. I couldn't control it.

A thought kept surfacing in my mind. *If all that I love were stripped away from me, would God truly be enough?* The question haunted me. I'd been banking on that truth my whole life. Test day had come, and I didn't know the answer.

In that moment, every external thing I heard and saw clicked into slow motion. Life started fading away into a world I could not reach and, I believed, could not reach me. The foundational question about God being enough thundered straight for me like a stampede of African rhinos. The louder it taunted, the more my uncertainty built.

As the closing prayer drew near, I had no idea how in Heaven's name I'd be able to stand up, let alone walk down the hall to my class.

With everyone's head bowed, amid prayers for this and that, my shaking escalated, becoming more uncontrollable. The desk beneath me held its stay as long as it could, but soon it began moving to the erratic rhythm of my fear. Any moment now, all my emotional willpower to remain calm would be gone, and I had no idea what would happen next.

Is this what it feels like to go crazy? I didn't know.

Suddenly, a gentle hand fell soft on my back. A soothing wave of compassion surged through my being, slowing down a torrent of fear, and initiating a calm stream of courage instead.

The shaking stopped.

Someone had reached through the dark veil and pulled me back to the present. No words. No solutions. No magic potions. She just touched me.

I peeked to see whose hand had ministered the relief. Ah, Jessica, our new student teacher. She occupied the desk next to me.

After prayer she asked, "Rebecca, are you alright? You were shaking."

My mind raced. *No. I'm not all right. My life is falling apart, and I'm not sure God will be sufficient.* I didn't say that. Instead I dodged the question and jumped straight to offering profuse thanks. Whatever I said appeased her—or scared her. She didn't ask any more questions.

Although I couldn't tell her at the time, Jessica was a hero to me that morning. She'll never know how God used her simple kindness to help me. Without her intervention, I'm not sure where the panic would have led.

Since that day, I've often wondered how the leprous man in Matthew 8 felt the day Jesus reached out and touched his disease-infested body. I imagine his experience mirrored mine—he wondered if anyone could make a difference, if hope still existed. After Jesus' miraculous touch, I bet that the man, like me, never again underestimated the power of human touch.

My circumstances had not changed one iota that day, but something else did, something more important. The window of belief that God sees me, knows me, and does not intend that I bear this burden alone cracked open just enough to let some cool air into my soul.

I also gained a glimpse of my utter weakness and the frailty of my solitary solutions. My inability to do this thing called life alone humbled me. God gently began convincing me that I needed help outside myself.

Up until this point in my life, I had no real experience in relying on others. While I loved people, I kept my troubles out of the conversations. This time around, I'd been silenced by two things: my desire to protect my husband's reputation, and the false notion that sharing personal struggles meant I didn't trust God. The Word says, "His grace is sufficient for me"[1]. So God and I could handle this on our own. After all, isn't that what spiritual people do?

Yes.

And no.

The Word also teaches us to "one another" each other: to exhort one another, to bear one another's burdens, to encourage one another, to strengthen one another. Shaking violently enough to make a desk rattle opened my eyes. Without some of that "one-anothering," I wouldn't make it.

≈∞≈

We needed community, not isolation. I needed to embrace a new idea; like the one Shannan Martin shares in her book *Falling Free*, "Sometimes surrender means letting go, and other times it means letting *in*."[2]

I hadn't learned that part yet, and I didn't have a clue where to begin.

God used my desperation to expose me to a new way of thinking and stretch me to unfamiliar territory. He knew my confused heart needed a push in the right direction, so He let me taste of the strength that can come from including others in your suffering. He didn't scold me for sharing my pain. He encouraged it.

Over time, I thoughtfully and carefully divulged my secret to a few key people in our lives. I needed them to know that our home resembled a ticking time bomb and I was wilting under the pressure of holding it steady. I needed someone to stand beside me while I deciphered how serious this extra-marital relationship was going to be. I didn't know yet. I needed their wisdom. And most of all, I needed them to intercede on our behalf.

Coming to the end of my own resources was a scary gift to receive. Though I had a long journey ahead, I saw glimpses of a beautiful treasure. Perhaps opening myself up to this season of grief and pain would bear delicious fruit.

WHAT I GAINED: I could not bear this pain alone, nor was that God's intention. I needed to reach out for help. And that's okay.

4

UNLOCKING A VAULTED HEART

The approaching Thanksgiving holiday haunted me.

The last few years, JP's basketball team had entered a tournament, making it impossible for us to travel any distance. So, my parents would drive up from North Florida to celebrate the weekend with us. Spending the holiday eating and watching basketball fit us perfectly.

But given the current situation, I needed a new holiday plan. Our house was too tiny to play happy couple for an entire weekend. No way could I hide our disastrous relationship from my parents in those tight quarters, and at this point, I didn't want to.

My mom and dad were the first ones I had *hinted* to about our marriage turmoil, but the extent of it wasn't the kind of information I wanted to convey over the phone. They loved JP like their own son. I needed to explain the situation face-to-face. I had done my best to protect his reputation with them, hoping life would smooth over before

I needed to come right out and say it, but it hadn't. My husband was slipping further and further away from me. It was time to come clean with them.

Heading to Florida for the weekend would be the perfect time to share my secret. Besides, I couldn't tell anyone else until I told the two people who loved me more than they loved their own lives.

But what would I say to the rest of my family and friends back home when I showed up without my husband? I wasn't ready for the whole world to know. I panicked at the thought of our failing marriage being the topic of discussion while family and friends cleared away the Thanksgiving dishes.

Plus, I didn't know what to do with the information myself, so how could I explain it to others? Call it denial. Call it shame. Either way, I needed a legitimate excuse that would safeguard JP's reputation, and buy me a little time to work it all out.

The excuse part was easy . . . and legitimate. JP had a basketball tournament and couldn't leave. It was true, and better yet, no one would question it. Everyone knew how much he loved coaching. At our wedding his groom's cake read, "God first, Rebecca second . . . and THEN comes basketball."

But even with my best effort to hold it together in front of everyone, how would I survive the relationship-infested holiday? I'd worn masks my whole life, but I didn't have one clever enough to conceal this ache for an entire weekend.

Time was running out. I needed something that would help me breathe normal breaths.

❦

The weekend before Thanksgiving, there we sat: my husband and I, in church, smiling and greeting all who ventured past our pew. JP's arm around my shoulder disguised the great gulf between us. I clung to the hope that an arm around me meant his renewed commitment to our life together instead of a life with *her*. But while I snuggled into his physical presence, his eyes remained vacant and his soul missing. My skin felt like it was being pricked with needles.

Waiting for the service to begin, an associate pastor reached out to shake JP's hand, his voice chipper and friendly. "How y'all doing today?"

My heart beat faster and I pleaded with my eyes. I wanted to scream, "Please help me! Don't buy my smile. We're not fine. No! Don't move on to the next couple. *Please . . .*"

But I didn't say that.

I did what respectable church members do and kept the pleasantries flowing. "Fine, how are you?"

So he, in turn, did what pastors do, and kept working the crowd. What choice did he have?

We were new to the church. Our previous experience in church leadership made us strong candidates for immediate service. We dressed the part and showed up when the doors were open. If this church functioned the way many do, the leadership had already discovered a list of duties we could perform should we decide to join. Little did they know our personal lives were like a house of cards, ready to collapse as soon as the air vent blew in our direction.

I've always loved church, and I've hungered for God most of my life. But these days, I entered the services with Dumbo-sized ears ready to hear any glimmer of hope, any word I could grasp to snap me from this frozen stupor. I needed something that no man could give me. I needed supernatural help and I knew it.

The last several weeks felt like I had landed on a schoolyard merry-go-round mid-spin. I'd tried to jump off, but couldn't get my bearings, leaving me no choice but to claw my way to the center of the ride and hold on for dear life, while the world twirled furiously around me.

This Sunday, my pastor's sermon acted like the friend who shows up to the playground, slows down the beastly ride, and at just the right moment, encourages you by shouting, "Jump!" My disoriented soul soaked in every word. His text came from 1 Thessalonians 5:18: "In everything give thanks, for this is the will of God in Christ Jesus concerning you."

I had heard the verse a hundred times. Probably one of the first ones I had ever memorized. But on this particular Sunday before Thanksgiving, it became the lost key to unlock the vault and warm my frozen, paralyzed condition.

He explained we're to give thanks *in* everything, not *for* everything. After all, not everything we experience is good.

That was a relief. I didn't see how I could thank God for the fact that my husband didn't want me anymore.

But the last part of the verse put a song in my silence. "This (giving thanks) is the will of God in Christ Jesus concerning you" (parenthesis mine).

While I didn't know much, I knew I yearned to be in God's will. But in my current state, I had no idea what that looked like anymore. I didn't know what to do, what to say, what not to do, what not to say. Should I leave JP? Should I stay?

I never dreamed I'd be at this crossroads. But this verse clearly stated what His will entailed for me. Simple. Give thanks *in*. I could do that.

෧෮

The certainty of knowing God's will infused me with a hope I hadn't known in weeks. At last, I knew one *sure* thing to do. I determined to focus on every obvious and random thing imaginable and thank God for them all.

My senses quickened now that I had somewhere other than my pain to focus my attention. I began immediately.

First off, I thanked Him that JP still went to church with me. Maybe God would capture his heart before it was too late. I stopped taking for granted that I had shoes to wear, a dress to put on, a car to get me where I needed to go, a Bible to read, a heated home, hot water, a blow dryer, a curling iron, hairspray, food in the pantry, TAB in the fridge. Oh, a fridge. Yes, I had a refrigerator. I didn't have to go to the laundromat anymore, and on and on.

❧

Choosing to give thanks amid the pain brought a new challenge my way. I questioned my ability to deal with reality and called myself names like "Pollyanna." I already battled the idea that I must be the most gullible person on earth to be fooled by JP's life, and I wondered if this was a good plan. I'd hear snarky remarks in my head like, *You're clueless. Look at you, scraping the bottom of the barrel to find things to be thankful for. Everyone can swallow, goofball.*

But I wasn't crazy. In fact, everyone couldn't swallow. I'd been guilty of taking daily gifts for granted. Swallowing, speaking, or walking was not some kind of right I had. I imagined how much more difficult life would be if I couldn't speak or walk. I thanked God all over again.

The pain in my heart still fought viciously for the attention. I waned and wobbled, but one truth made the difference; the fact that "*This* is the will of God" spurred me on to accept God's grace and choose His will. God would never require of me something I couldn't do. He always has my best interest at heart. So, if His will meant giving thanks, then by golly, I would press on.

That Thanksgiving weekend, I shared my secret with my mom and dad. They listened with compassion and grace. Once that burden was off my heart, the whole thankfulness mindset carried me into a surprisingly pleasant and enjoyable holiday, an absolute miracle to me. Like Ann

Voskamp says in *One Thousand Gifts*, "We don't have to change what we see. Only the way we see."[1]

Giving thanks in all things reminded me I still had wonderful people in my life to enjoy and love. And enjoy and love I did.

Over the next several months, loneliness sent me to Florida on several weekends to be with my parents. I truly experienced a thankful heart and learned to relish the time alone with my mom and dad. In their presence, I found chunks of my soul that had been damaged or stolen, and their home provided a safe respite from the pain.

Recognizing and appreciating blessings absolutely did not remedy the problem or answer all the queries. The hurt still existed. The confusion still haunted. The dark clammy pit still engulfed. But thankfulness provided a perspective and reprieve from the barrage of negative realities. It deposited truth into the balance and pumped little breaths of air into my gasping soul.

WHAT I GAINED: Giving thanks was not the whole answer, but like the edge pieces of a jigsaw puzzle, it provided a framework on which to build.

5

LIFEJACKET FOR ONE

Thanksgiving night the phone rang. It was JP.

"Hello Beck. I just wanted to let you know your sister called looking for you guys." His voice sounded humble and apologetic.

That felt like an odd reason for a call. "Yeah, thanks. We talked to her."

"Uh . . . are you going to be back in time for my game tomorrow night? We play at 7:00."

My heart caught in my throat. I moved the phone away from my mouth to take a deep breath. *Was he as miserable without me as I was without him?* I tried to keep my voice even. "I'll see." Then I hung up the phone.

My mind reeled. Was this time to play hard to get or prove to him I'd walk barefoot to get there if he wanted me to?

I sought my mom's advice. She assured me this was a

good sign and said, "By all means, you should go."

Excited but guarded, I gathered my things and headed home. I couldn't wait to see him, and it sounded as if he felt the same way. This was one more check in the all-of-this-was-just-a-phase column. It would be over soon. Hallelujah.

I envisioned the big bear hug I'd give him and began rehearsing all the details I wanted to share with him about my weekend in Florida.

❧

Walking into the gym that night, I flashed him a smile as we made eye contact, but his eyes passed over me as if I was no more than a random fan in the stands. Not a grin. Not a nod of the head. Nothing. I sensed all my positive, warm fuzzy thoughts boarding a one-way flight to Siberia.

No. I'll give him the benefit of the doubt. I know how single-minded a coach can be before a game. I could handle that.

But after the game, as his team exited the locker room to watch the rest of the tournament, he stalled several minutes before heading my direction. The tension inside me mounted. JP had clearly invited me here, but when he finally made it to my bleacher seat, he barely said hello before he dashed from one spot to the other, leaving only awkwardness and humiliation to keep me company. Apparently, my bear hug would have to wait.

While I waved to a few acquaintances, my mind scrambled to calm my thoughts and figure out what was happening. Why had he asked me to come? Maybe his new girl had shown up unexpectedly? I tried to scan the gym with the subtleness of an undercover agent, hoping my glances weren't suspicious.

I never saw her.

I wanted out of that gym, but my deep desire to restore our relationship cemented me to those bleachers. I didn't want to give him a moment's doubt about my desire for our marriage to survive, even if it meant embarrassment and discomfort.

And it would.

After the tournament, despite icy roads and the fact that I hadn't seen him in several days, I discovered he had no intention of riding home with me. He sent me on my way like a child being pushed off to boarding school by a rogue parent. He instead chose to ride the almost empty bus home.

Once again, I'd made myself vulnerable. I'd changed my plans because I thought he missed me. Instead, humiliation had won the night, not to mention the cold-hard fact that JP and I were traveling further apart. And I seemed to be the only one of us not enjoying the trip.

⌇

As the days droned by, I pictured myself treading water. With my head above the surface, I smiled and carried on my daily routine as if all was right in the world, while beneath the water, I kicked and paddled with all my might to stay afloat.

Every time the hopelessness threatened to drown me, God cranked up His mercy in unexplainable ways, ways that sound bizarre apart from Him.

❧

Each year, our teaching staff committed to playing the hand bells for one of our school programs. Most of us had some form of musical training, and none of us had a desire to do anything half-heartedly.

Carving out practice time required a sacrifice for most of the staff, but I relished the hour. For a few moments, I escaped from reality and lost myself in the land of musical notes and rhythms. The sense of accomplishment and the sweet music invigorated my being like a dip in the pool on a scorching day.

One day, I pulled into the parking lot a few minutes early for practice. While I normally loved rehearsal, this day I had no strength. The prospective future loomed heavy, and the devastation that my husband didn't want me anymore squeezed my heart like a vice. I didn't know if I had the gumption to walk the hundred steps into the building.

I opened my car door hoping the beautiful weather and cool breeze would infuse a little relief into my soul. My body literally ached to be touched and cradled.

Suddenly, I heard a strange noise approaching my car from the rear. I leaned my body out of the door to see what made the sound. A yellow cat charged towards me as if he were king of the jungle.

I don't like cats.

Before I knew what hit me, that cat leaped into my lap. My first instinct was to shoo the fur ball away. But before I could gather my wits, the feline sat back and walked its front paws up my chest. Big green eyes gazed straight into mine as it gently padded its little paws all over my weary face. Then he'd take a break and rub his fluffy head up against my neck and purr. After a few soft head butts, he'd repeat with the paws and then again with the snuggling. I hadn't felt a touch so comforting in days.

My mind fluttered. *I should push the cat out.* But the soft touching intoxicated me.

Before I knew it, the cat bolted away as quickly as it had appeared. When I regained my senses, I turned to see which way he fled. I saw nothing, as if the cat disappeared into thin air. Soaking in what had happened, I sat stunned. It wasn't a human touch, but the soft cuddles revived my insides.

I have no idea where that cat came from or where he disappeared to afterwards.

Call me crazy, but I know God sent it. In that moment I felt Him whisper to me, "Rebecca, I see you. JP may have abandoned you, but I never will. I know how your heart aches, and I care about you, my darling."

I'd need that reminder in the days ahead.

My life with JP, and hence my future, hung suspended like a piñata waiting for the next blow. I could only hope that by some miracle it would be lowered back to the ground without permanent damage. But in all likelihood, more blows would come, disfiguring us beyond recognition.

Earlier in our relationship JP and I had grappled with the

threat of other women: occasional wandering eyes, a few suspiciously close friendships with ladies, odd charges on our credit card. But when confronted with them, his explanations sounded logical and innocent. None of it lasted long and nothing to this level of betrayal. An agonizing chunk of wait-time needed to pass before I could discern if this was another passing phase, or if he planned on burning bridges and embracing this new lifestyle. We were dizzy with problems and needed someone to help us decipher where we were headed.

JP agreed to meet one-on-one with a pastor friend. Both Jon and his wife Liz Anne adored us. They were not afraid to address tough issues, and they understood God's grace to forgive and restore. Pastor Jon embraced JP with sympathy and viewed him as a weakened brother in need of restoration.

I knew this meeting was pivotal. Jon's compassion and nonjudgmental spirit would not dissuade him from addressing the gravity of the situation. He would shoot straight, give JP practical steps toward making this right and love him every step of the way. I tried to keep my insides calm as I waited for JP to return home.

After the meeting, JP and I sat in our living room and talked about our lives as if we were discussing a random news story. Both of us, calm and unemotional. He confessed things he'd never told me. He had indeed been physically unfaithful to me and this wasn't the first time.

This wasn't the first time?

My mind flash backed as he shared the details. *How could*

I be so stupid, so naïve? All those times we had together, *what had they been?* He proceeded to tell me, "Beck, I don't want to hurt you. I don't know how I feel about this other woman. No, I'm not leaving Wilson High. And yes, I know we need counseling."

In some ways, bits of relief nestled in my heart. If JP chose to continue in this lifestyle, his unfaithfulness meant I had scriptural grounds for divorce. It's not what I wanted. I would have followed JP to the farthest reaches of the earth if he'd be willing to make things right.

Although I never expected this type of crisis to happen to me, I always thought I'd know what to do if I discovered my husband had been unfaithful. My girlfriends and I had discussed our bold solutions—should we ever face such a dilemma—wearing big-girl panties and self-righteous halos. Theories flew from our lips like coaching tips from fans in the bleachers. We meant well at the time, but I was learning how drastically your perspective changes when you find yourself suited up and holding the ball.

I still couldn't read JP. He confessed, but he didn't seem remorseful.

I took my next cue from Pastor Jon. He never broke JP's confidence, but his attitude toward him had dramatically shifted. One day he explained, "Rebecca, if JP was a member of our church, he'd be taken off our membership roll."

I knew what that meant. JP had no intention of repenting from his sin.

❦

There are times and seasons for everything. God's word tells us as much, that there's "a time to break down, and a time to build up; a time to weep, and a time to laugh; a time to mourn, and a time to dance; a time to cast away stones, and a time to gather stones together; a time to embrace, and a time to refrain from embracing; a time to get, and a time to lose; a time to keep, and a time to cast away."[1]

I get that.

Right now was time to do something. If only I knew what. I'd spent the last several weeks waiting, praying, assessing, unsure what direction our lives would take. As Christmas neared, I sensed the hands of time changing from waiting to action.

After weeks of seeking God and paying close attention to JP's actions and reactions, I narrowed my focus down to two main pursuits. The first one involved the survival of our marriage. I'd gathered enough information to realize that the current path hurled our marriage towards destruction. If I hoped for survival, we needed to make some drastic changes.

My second objective didn't involve JP at all. I wanted to know God more and seek His will for my life. JP's choices couldn't stop me from pursuing God's heart and being obedient to His leading. I rested in that assurance.

The two pursuits represented the difference between a goal and a desire. A goal is something I can reach for regardless of what another person does, while a desire is something I want but can't control. I could *desire* for our marriage to be restored, but since a healthy marriage required my husband's participation, I couldn't pursue it like a goal. Understanding that principle helped me. While I desired a restored marriage, seeking God became my goal.

⁓

Christmas break approached. As I slipped out of class and into my Camry, I headed once again to Florida, alone. I hated leaving JP over another holiday, but I looked forward to a reprieve from the daily duties of teaching to focus all my attention on pressing into God.

As I sought His direction, He gave me a vivid mental picture:

I envisioned JP and me floating in the middle of large lake. A small boat hovered in the distance with the shore barely visible. JP and I were both treading water to stay afloat, but as our strength waned, we started to sink.

I called to God, "Help!"

Instantly, a lifejacket appeared. I held on to one side and thrust the other toward JP, but when he grabbed ahold of it, his extra weight pulled us down below the surface. We sputtered back above the water line and gasped for a breath before the cold water could swallow us again.

My determination kept us above water for a while, but finally I faced the facts. No matter how hard I struggled to keep us afloat, my lifejacket proved only sufficient for one. *Why wouldn't JP just ask God for his own life preserver?* I knew God had one ready for him. But I also realized that no matter how desperately I wanted it for him, the request must come from his own lips.

I grabbed his shoulders and shouted my request from the depths of my being. "Just ask for the dang preserver. Don't you see what you're doing here?"

He responded with the gusto of a dead fish.

Then the force of my anger crumbled into sobs because I knew. He didn't ask for the lifejacket because he didn't want it. Didn't want me, either.

The longer we splashed and kicked the clearer the choice became. The rescue boat circled close. We bobbed from its wake and the gasoline smell filled the air. A rope dangled from its rear just within my reach.

Decision time.

If I grabbed onto the rope, the boat would tug me safely to shore. But that would mean leaving JP alone in the water, not knowing what would become of him. If I let go of the rope, I could stay here with him treading water. With that plan, eventually we would both drown.

If my goal entailed pursuing God's heart, then I needed to hold on to the rope and get to the shore. Hopefully, if I stopped enabling JP to stay afloat, he'd eventually call out for his own lifejacket.

I grabbed the line from the boat. JP did not.

I imagined that one day in the future I'd sense someone watching me. I'd scan the crowd to see JP, bright-eyed and strong, making his way my direction. He'd gather me in his arms and thank me for loving him enough to do the hard thing.

This last picture coincided with the same idea my counselor explained to me about writing JP's name on a piece of paper and letting God take it. But the paper exercise required only mental release. Time had come for a major step. Physical separation.

If I had any hope of our marriage surviving, I needed to stop enabling his unhealthy behavior. God used the lifejacket picture to infuse enough courage in my soul to face the reality of living separately. I needed to trust that my Sovereign God was plenty capable of taking care of John Parker Smith.

Separating not only required details and living arrangements I couldn't begin to think about, but it also forced me to publicly admit the gaping holes in our marriage. People would find out, and I wouldn't be able to protect his reputation anymore.

What would I tell my friends? I didn't want everyone to hate him.

Playing the Devil's advocate, I battled whether I even wanted to go this route. Unfortunately, I knew of women whose husbands danced with infidelity, and yet the couple played the role of fine, upstanding family. It baffled me.

These dear wives slid into a survival mode daze, doing their best to appear fine on the outside. But inside, they existed as a brittle skeleton. Not exactly the abundant life God planned. Some spewed bitterness and defensiveness at every turn, and some resembled a nervous basket case holding it together by a thread. And who wouldn't be. Their husbands seemed fine with the sham, as long as the wife didn't interfere with his shenanigans.

Perhaps I could go that route. Forget the whole thing

ever happened. I could picture JP being content to live that facade. Apparently, he'd been living that lie off and on for years.

But true love always acts in the best interest of another, even if those actions make your loved one mad. I loved JP with all my heart. His chosen path defied God's purpose and plan for his life. I couldn't sit by and enable his self-destruction. I desired for him to know God's peace and experience the blessings of a clean life.

The sweep-it-under-the-rug option wouldn't fly. Not only for JP's sake, but my sanity couldn't survive the ugly cover-up either. My insides were shriveling fast.

I had a ton of questions and no idea what the journey ahead would bring. I hoped my actions would force JP to realize the consequences of his choices, but I also understood that tough love doesn't always turn out the way one hopes. He may remain unaffected by my actions and choose to walk away from this marriage without so much as a glance over his shoulder.

Regardless, the time to watch and wait was over. Time to move.

WHAT I GAINED: There may come a time when walking away is the most loving act one can do.

6

SNEAK ATTACK

Christmas break ended, along with the life I once knew.

Details of my new living arrangements began falling into place during my two-week visit to Florida. Several weeks earlier, based on the principles of *Love Must Be Tough* by James Dobson, and after discussing it with my parents, I asked JP to leave. I explained that I loved him too much to enable his lifestyle. Since he was the one who broke our covenant, he should be the one to leave. I thought he'd agree it was only fair.

Instead, he threw his head back and laughed. "What are you going to do? Throw me out?"

Shocked at his reaction, a nervous laugh escaped my lips. He had a valid point. I couldn't physically force him out if he wasn't willing to go. It was a stupid plan, and we both knew it.

Suddenly, his laughter stopped. His eyes locked onto

mine and he said, "Besides, where would I go?"

It took me a minute to realize he was serious. *What? What do you mean, where would you go? How about your work buddies or that great little woman you've got?*

As if reading my mind, his eyes dropped, and his tone sounded more somber than I'd heard in a long time. "Rebecca, if I went to the places that would take me in, I don't know what would happen to me. They're bad. I don't think I'd make it out of there."

His statement took me back. Was he admitting he was trapped and trying to get out? Confusion, mixed with a hope that deep down he rejected his current lifestyle, ricocheted across my mind.

One thing was sure. He had *no* intention of vacating our cozy little nest. If I wanted to demonstrate tough love, I would have to be the one to leave.

At times, my resolve toward this new stage in fighting for our marriage resembled the determination of a freight train barreling down the tracks. But in a flash, panic would overwhelm me and make me wonder, *"What on earth am I going to do?"* I fought the urge to stay in my little bungalow and pretend this never happened. But I knew that wasn't an option, not if I hoped for us to be whole again.

Just when I'd feel like giving up, God would reveal another detail and courage would reappear. For starters, a friend of a friend rented me a room for several days until I could assess my new situation; and my fellow teachers and the school board members offered to take up a monthly collection to help counterbalance my new expenses. As devastating as JP's actions had been, the sacrificial care my Crestview School community expressed on my behalf amazed me. Troubled me, actually.

The thought of accepting others' hard-earned cash felt wrong. I believed God would provide; I just hadn't anticipated my friends footing the bill. I needed my dad's guidance before I could agree to this new plan of action.

One day, when I was home I asked. "Dad, is it okay for me to accept these generous offers?"

I'll never forget his response. He said, "Rebecca, that's exactly what the body of Christ is supposed to do."

Soon, I discovered God's plan for my survival included receiving an ocean more than I could ever return. Part of His scraping the gunk out of my life meant not only humbling myself enough to admit I needed help, but also accepting the gifts He provided, in whatever means He chose to provide them.

❧

With my return plan in place, on New Year's Day I drove back to Georgia with the same terror and thrill as standing for the first time in the high-dive line at the local swimming pool.

I should have been furious with JP, and at times I wanted to punch him until I had no more strength. But absence has a magical way of refreshing and exaggerating good memories. And after his description of his new friends, I believed God was opening his eyes to reality without me.

As I traveled back, listening to the football games on the

radio drew me to him. We always watched sports together. I just knew in my heart, *"He must be thinking of me. We've shared too much history for him not to be."* My eyes sparkled. Oh, how I hoped it to be true. The thought thrust me forward mile by mile.

But the leading contribution to my light heart belonged to the fact that I had just leaped forward on the biggest step of faith I had ever taken. My unknown future hadn't paralyzed me from doing what God put in my heart to do. In my gut, I *knew* this separation, although necessary, would be temporary. In the end, our marriage would be stronger than it ever could have been without this debacle. One day I'd look back and thank God for all of it.

～∘◦∘～

Before I could go to my new residence, I needed to drop by the house to gather a few things. I was glad for the excuse to see JP. Somewhere in my subconscious, I concocted an imaginary scene.

JP would beg me not to go. I'd see tenderness in those baby blue eyes. He'd ask me, "How are you, Beck? I miss you."

I'd lower my head and pick at my fingernails. Then peek up. Tell him I miss him, too.

We would break down the day's football games and discuss his basketball team. When the conversation died down a little, he'd say, "Will you tell me where you're staying? Or at least assure me it's safe," his tone not even trying to mask his concern.

I'd be vague, all the while secretly hoping he'd figure it out.

"When do you plan on coming home?" He'd brush a strand of hair from my face. "You know I can't sleep well when we're apart."

Then he'd say he understood why I was leaving, but maybe we could run over to the new chicken place up the street and grab a bite to eat before I left.

He would ask me all that, but I would remain strong. I'd tell him, "I love you desperately JP, and that's why I cannot stay; but yes . . . I guess we could get something to eat first."

Somewhere in my subconscious that scene broadcasted in vibrant HD.

Walking up the concrete steps and onto our little front porch comforted me. My heart quickened as I grasped the metal doorknob.

Unlocked.

As I stepped inside, an unfamiliar, acrid odor snatched my breath. In an instant, every pleasantry I had focused on during my five-hour drive screeched to a halt. I blurted out, "What is that awful smell?"

Just a few weeks ago my cottage sang bright and cheery. Today, however, with the blinds drawn tight, darkness assaulted me. Not only a physical darkness, but also an oppressive heaviness hung thick in the air. My home had transformed from welcoming and happy to suffocating and foreign.

As my eyes adjusted, I noticed strange gadgets had now replaced my mantel wreath and pictures. I should have investigated. I didn't. I walked on past, trying to assess them, but not too intently, as if my ignorance could eliminate the reality of their intended use.

But it was my husband's aloof, dazed expression that emerged from the shadows and slapped me across the face. Not exactly the welcome wagon I'd concocted. He mumbled from the couch that he didn't know what the smell was. (He lied.) And he'd ask the landlord to check into it.

I grabbed a few things and fled back to the Camry, my new safe place. In an instant, my car became the only place that wouldn't shoo me away or wonder how long I planned to stay.

Safe in the car, I found Truth sitting in the passenger's seat. It needed to say something, and I needed to listen. My husband knew I was back in town. He knew I wasn't coming home. Not only did he *not* ask me to stay, but most telling of all, I sensed his relief when I left.

Despite the disenchanted homecoming, escaping that awful environment refreshed my spirit. A safe place awaited me, and I had transportation to get there. But best of all, the sweet presence of Jesus covered me like a canopy.

Driving to the lady's home, I remembered the lifejacket scenario and God's abundant provision. His Spirit comforted me. Peace returned. I thanked Him repeatedly that I didn't have to stay in that oppressive house tonight. One day it would transform back to my happy bungalow, and I'd return home. Just not today.

◠◡◠

My new hostess, Grace, explained she'd be out of town for several days, but left word for me to, "Make myself at home." I found the spare bedroom furnished with a bare mattress and box spring. No sheets. No blanket. I briefly considered being depressed when I saw my new space, but after my recent experience, what did it matter if the bed had no sheets? It was a bed, and it was away from that awful place I used to call home.

How I made it through the next days, I'm not sure. My emotions resembled live wires lying near a puddle of water. Trying to set up some kind of home in a strange environment and realizing my total dependence on people's generosity heightened the reality of my situation, making it more real than I wanted to admit. But I had counted the cost. I knew life would be challenging if I chose to love JP enough to reject his current lifestyle. That much I expected.

But I hadn't expected what came next.

In a matter of hours, everything I ever believed about God— about Who He is and my relationship with Him— threatened to collapse. I faced the deepest onslaught of doubt and confusion I'd known to date. It felt like trying to hold off a tsunami with my niece's Hello Kitty umbrella.

Many times in the past several weeks, I had asked myself, "How'd I end up *here*?" But deep down, I aimed that question at God. Being alone in an unfamiliar place, my heart unleashed a battery of confrontational questions I could no longer avoid. Forehead wrinkled. Lips pressed. My tone aghast. I asked, *"How could You let me marry this man? Why didn't You warn me?"*

Since I was a little girl, I wanted nothing more than a God-honoring life and home. Growing up, I practiced all kinds of safeguards to guarantee a godly marriage: dating only Christians, vowing to barely kiss a guy until we were married. I thought those elements ensured marriage success.

But it wasn't working out like that at all. Confusion tracked me like a heat-seeking missile. I'd spent hours praying for JP, even before I met him. I had begged God to help me to marry the right man. How could He *betray* me like this? I'd trusted Him to watch my back. What did I have to show for it? Nothing, but a shattered life.

These questions clawed out a wretched pit being prepared for me.

∽◦◦◦∽

The following Sunday I decided to try a ladies' Sunday school class at my new church. The teacher's dynamic reputation prodded me to hunt down her room and enter the large group.

I wore my favorite dress, hoping that if I looked nice, I'd conjure up enough bravado to combat my quivering spirit. The thought of meeting a horde of chatty women or speaking a bunch of churchy lingo seemed impossible today. I had no clue how to introduce myself or what box to check on the visitor slip. Shoot, I didn't even know my address. Somehow, I slid in unnoticed and managed to find a secluded spot in the back row.

I still remember the lesson—a twist on Paul's leadership I'd never considered. I soaked it in, thanking God that I'd made it to class, and maybe this would be okay.

Then without warning, it came. The teacher jumped off the trail to address women who blame God for the man they married.

My ears perked. My stomach flipped. She continued, "Don't tell me you or your parents didn't have a check in your spirit when you married him . . ."

Suddenly, I felt myself freefalling into a black hole. The world started spinning as my mind raced back to my wedding day. *Is that why I was so miserable?*

⚬

JP accepted Christ right before we started dating, and as a new believer he possessed a ton of rough edges. As our relationship deepened, I began an agonizing dialogue with God about marrying JP, unsure if our relationship should continue. I could barely pick out a new outfit, let alone decide on a life's mate.

No one advised me against marrying him. In fact, the counsel I received encourage me to weigh JP based on his growth. Was he perfect? No. But neither was I. Did he appear to be growing? Well . . . most of the time.

The day I committed my heart to JP, his actions had hurt my feelings yet again. He called it play, but I felt the embarrassment of subtle rejection. Nothing life altering, just enough to wonder if he would ever embody the words "cherish and protect." I thought unconditional love made it my duty to bear it. No one is perfect.

So that day, while playing whiffle ball, I decided. I'd

accept the good, the bad and the ugly because that's what godly relationships did. A few months later, he knelt before me and asked me to be his wife. With a clear conscience from God and a committed heart, I said yes.

During the six months of wedding preparations, I teetered between anticipation and dread. On the dread days, I scolded myself because I'd already wrestled this out with God. The stern rebuke reminded, "Love isn't based on feeling. Quit flip-flopping back and forth. You've prayed about who you'd marry since you were old enough to understand. God will protect you. He's blocked other relationships from flourishing, but not this one, so no more doubting."

Okay. Geez.

Unfortunately, the dress rehearsal landed on a dread day. Instead of feeling giddy and excited, I moved through the motions like a puppet, laughing and smiling right on cue. But inside, the stark reality of forever with this man—who disappointed me so often—haunted me through our mock ceremony. Then confusion and guilt berated me, and I feared my expectations had landed me in the hard-to-please category, or an unattainable fantasy world.

The wedding day came accompanied by a drizzling rain that resembled someone spitting in your face. And truth be told, the weather reflected the angst in my heart. But I determined to slip into costume and act like this was the "happiest day of my life."

Uh, not.

Stephanie, one of my bridesmaids, beamed and said,

"This must be like Christmas morning!" Instead of a big grin, big tears gushed down my face. This experience had turned out nothing like I'd imagined. Stephanie grabbed my hands and prayed, unsure what else to do. Her prayer eased my heart, yet inside my mind questioned. *I didn't think it was supposed to be like this. No one ever told me I'd feel such dread. Maybe no one else does. It's just me. I'm a quack.*

In that moment, it suddenly dawned on me that I had no guarantee JP would always love me. I knew my parents would never abandon me. But this man . . . What if he changed his mind one day?

I'd heard of wedding jitters, but never understood what it meant. I concluded *I'm just wishy-washy. This whole experience must be a classic example of cold feet.* It must be. So, I shoved down the doubts, smiled bright and said, "I do."

❦

Sitting in that Sunday school classroom, these thoughts flooded my memory. It never occurred to me before now that the uncertainty I felt that day could have been the Holy Spirit. If this relationship was so wrong, wasn't it a little late for the prompting? Wouldn't my warning consist of more than a bad feeling just hours before I marched down the aisle?

And now, after almost a decade of marriage, I adored being my husband's wife. No one could love a person more than I loved JP Smith. Had he hurt me deeply? Absolutely. But I did not regret marrying him. I often said of our wedding day, "If I had known then what I know now, I would have enjoyed the day much more." But now my new Sunday school teacher insinuated that those feelings were warnings from the Holy Spirit, and I simply didn't bother to listen.

My heart cried out, *"Is this true, God? Could it be that I missed the most prayed about decision of my life because I didn't listen? And if that's true, maybe I've never listened to You. Did I betray You? I'm devastated if I did. I thought I loved you, God . . .*

Confusion blindfolded my thoughts, and then spun me dizzy. It felt like God betrayed *me*, yet He wasn't capable of such actions. That left all fingers pointing back in my direction.

Alarm pulsed through my veins. I could barely breathe.

I don't trust myself. Oh, Father, my heart longs for you. I love you. Yet, how could I really love you and then make this mistake for my life's mate? I'm so confused.

It was one thing to be deserted by JP, but to be cut off from communion with my God? I *absolutely* couldn't bear it.

Thus, the spiritual attack began.

With everything I ever *thought* I believed hanging in the balance, somehow I made it from church back to Grace's house. My whole life had been built on my relationship with God, and yet what I heard in the Sunday school class suggested that I didn't have a clue how to hear God's voice. Was my whole life a charade? The shock of such a prospect flung me around like a rag doll in a tornado. Satan had kicked his steal-kill-destroy method into high gear aimed at my already trembling knees.

And then the phone rang.

It was my mother. She knew me as well as anyone on earth. I couldn't even try to act brave. My voice cracked as I relived the whole morning out loud.

Mom listened. Then she said, "Rebecca, I promise you. This is Satan's attack to bring confusion and isolation. I won't stand for it."

Her voice took on the authority of a queen on her throne, and she prayed. "Oh Father, I love you. Right now, in the name of Jesus, I pray for Your blood to cover Rebecca from the top of her head down to the very tips of her toes. You are not the author of confusion, God. On the authority of Your cross, I demand the devil out. There is no room for him here. I pray that he would leave her alone this instant. And God, let Your love wrap her up like a warm blanket. In Jesus' name, amen."

My heart rate slowed as I focused on her words.

My mom's devoted love reminded me of the verse in Matthew that says, *"If you then who are evil, know how to give good gifts to your children, how much more will your Father who is in heaven give good things to those who ask him!"*[1] I knew my parents loved me. How much more did my Heavenly Father love.

That Sunday night I decided to try a church closer to my new prospective home. My friend Heather knew the pastor and recommended I try it. Maybe this church would be the perfect fresh start.

I could picture it. I'd walk in the vestibule. Sweet music would fill the space, as a spotlight shone down from heaven. People, faces filled with anticipation, would be lined up waiting to welcome me into their community, take me under their wings and nurture me back to strength.

Wrong. *Cue rejection music.*

Instead, "weirdo" must have been stamped on my forehead. *Add the womp-womp sound effect here.* People acknowledged my presence by glares and stares, not sure what to do with a creature like me. My fancy dress and high heels stuck out among the jeans and boots that filled the lobby. *Nice.* Exhausted, I wondered what I was doing here.

My questions grew when they announced that the preacher I'd come to hear was out of town. In his place, one of their "preacher boys" commandeered the pulpit. The young man's zeal and effort to impress made it difficult to take him seriously.

Soon his sermon led to sharing his testimony. His southern accent decorated his point, "My wife had no business datin' a dude like me."

My attention snapped into focus.

"She claimed Christ. I claimed you-only-go-around-once and lived a heathen lifestyle to prove it. Mothers cringed to see their daughters dating a creep like me, let alone marry me."

Yet, marry they did. Later, God saved him and then called him to preach.

Instead of rejoicing at God's mercy, anger stomped

around in my heart. *God, how is that fair? This chick dated someone she KNEW denied you, yet she married him anyway. Now, he gets saved, and she gets to be a preacher's wife. I would've loved being a preacher's wife. I've begged for Your guidance since I was a little girl. I've never wanted to live outside of your presence. No man is worth that. I love you too much. Yet, whoop-de-doo! Look at me! I've been abandoned. Rejected. And what's my prize for seeking You? A broken heart smeared all over the carpet.*

I absolutely didn't understand.

On the last syllable of amen, I shot out the doors and headed to my car. I couldn't wait to get out of there, but I couldn't go home to an empty house, a bed with no sheets and a pile of unanswered questions. Instead, I wandered around a K-mart in a stupor, trying to convince myself it would be fun to pick out a new bedspread. That was a hard sell since my immense desire involved going back to my former home, curling up in my own soft bed and pretending none of this had ever happened.

I kept telling myself that everything was going to be just fine, all the while fighting the urge to start sobbing in the center aisle, *"Can't anyone see I'm dying over here. Please. Would someone just give me a hug?"*

This doozy of a day, full of raging emotions and downright dirty battle, left me stranded on a tightrope of despair strung across a deep ravine of doubt and confusion.

Then a thought dawned on me: perhaps my attendance at that country church was no accident, but rather a gracious appointment by God.

My Father God visited that Sunday school class with me,

rode home next to me and knew every doubt and question tormenting me. He also knew the pastor of the country church would be out and the young whippersnapper would preach in his stead. He knew the man would share his testimony. And He definitely didn't mean for the preacher's story of mercy to hurt me.

No. He meant it to encourage me, to tell me, "Rebecca, honey, don't you see? Even if you had been rebellious towards me, I'd still be able to make it right. I know you don't understand. You cannot at this point. Just know that this is not happening because you've been living in rebellion and disobedience to Me."

I've learned a lot since that hellish day. Yes, *hellish*. I'd place that day next to the night I discovered my husband didn't want me anymore. That Sunday in January, I thought I'd lost God. I came within a hair's breadth of believing that I'd built my whole life on a make-believe relationship with Him, which is exactly what the Enemy of my soul wanted me to think.

Satan is no joke. He is cruel and hits us when we're weak. He almost convinced me that I had no clue who God is, that I'd never recognized His voice and that I had no business trusting Him. He knew if he swayed me into buying that lie, I'd be crippled for life.

I don't claim to understand why God permits Satan to have such access to our lives, but I find hope in a principle I heard Beth Moore say. She reminded her Bible class that while Satan is allowed to sift us as wheat, our Father will never allow him to sift us any more than what God will use to strengthen and purify us.

Satan may appear to have control and present himself as the victor. But I John 4:4 says, "Greater is He that is in me, than he that is in the world!" My God will come. He will rescue me from the jaws of the Enemy's schemes and then leverage his tactics for my advantage.

Now that's what I call a sneak attack.

WHAT I GAINED: I realized I have an enemy, and he doesn't play fair. But God is greater and will always have the last word.

7

DON'T QUIT ONE STREET
TOO EARLY

School started the next day, and I wanted to play hooky . . .
for the rest of the year.

The temptation to quit sometimes felt like a downright
necessity—the hurt too intense or the conflict too complex. I
longed for a path with less resistance.

Truth is, I could kiss my parents' feet for instilling in my
siblings and me not to quit. If we started something, we kept
at it. When circumstances turned rocky or a better
opportunity came along, we stuck with our commitment to
the end—with a good attitude. And I'm forever grateful.

My new financial burdens and wondering where I'd lay
my head each night added to the daily battle for mere
survival. Suddenly, mindless tasks like going to the grocery
store or cleaning the toilet required the stamina of walking
up a downward moving escalator. I wished I could shake off
this disaster, but no amount of longing could free me from

it.

The separation left me feeling detached from friends and my church family. I had no idea where I should live. I felt utterly dependent on others to provide for my needs. My husband didn't want me. And, oh yeah, I was still unsure if I had offended God or not. It only made sense that my professional life should join the mêlée.

I played school as a child, and now that I taught for a living, teaching fit me like a great pair of jeans. But this year made me wonder if I'd been snatched from earth and transported into another galaxy.

Overall, my class measured on the extremely gifted side, but the mix of classroom personalities screamed disaster. I hated the educator I'd become. I scolded this class more in the first five minutes of the day than my past classes received in a whole semester.

Each day, I found myself in the middle of a massive power struggle—with a bunch of first graders. Often, my little brood ran over my best efforts of classroom control. Some days I won. Most days I lost.

The ringleader, Cassie, was a child with the most intense ADHD I had ever witnessed. Yet even in her disruptions, her bright, creative mind left me stunned at the complexity of her intellect. However, to my great disadvantage, along with that mind came a sharp wit. In a breath, her quick comments could send the class into a cackling frenzy, typically with me as the laughingstock.

One morning, Cassie made a comment that made even the pliable children giggle uncontrollably. Add to the scene a scowling adult barking out, "That is *not* funny." Even if the comment wasn't sidesplitting, me sounding once again like the proverbial monster-teacher made it one.

On this day, every time I tried bringing the class to order, Cassie responded with a comment more hilarious than the last time. The more she rebutted, the more I huffed, the funnier it became.

At some point, my normal-self caught a glimpse of the monster-self. Before I knew it, the whole crazy scene had managed not only to tickle my funny bone, but downright attack it.

It started gurgling in my depths. I held my breath. I turned my head. But I could feel it rising in my chest. I crossed my arms. I pursed my lips. I tried everything possible to keep from joining the skirmish.

Finally, I couldn't take it anymore. It started with a throaty cough. Then, laughter erupted from my depths, filling every square inch of the room: the out of control-tears running down your face-can't breathe-bent over slapping your leg like a drum-kind of laughter that wobbles on the edge of a full-blown meltdown. The children squealed with delight, and I relished every second of it. I needed to enjoy the moment because the rest of the day would be lost.

Sure enough, for the remainder of the day control belonged to them. And they knew it. For me, the joy of the moment was short-lived.

This group of six-year-olds managed to smash, stomp

and obliterate any minuscule fragment of self-esteem I might have had remaining. The mountain of duty and failure I faced each day felt like trying to peddle a bike backwards up a hill.

Without God in the picture, I understood why people go off the deep end with pills and booze. The pain and loneliness, along with the sheer burden of survival, shrouded my moments with dread and weariness. I wanted to give up on this step of faith. Things would be simpler if I went back to Florida and cocooned myself in my parents' home.

But a question disturbed me: what if I gave up too soon? JP may be on the verge of a major heart-change. What if I quit before that breakthrough?

JP wasn't the only one on the verge of breakthrough. Under the tutelage of the Crestview community, I started blossoming and tasting the sweetness of God in a way I never knew existed. I longed for more. In all probability, taking the easy way out would've required sticking God back in the small box I'd fabricated for Him. I couldn't bear the thought.

But peering into the future, my spirit crumbled at the sorrow and responsibility ahead.

⸎

Just a few days into the new year, questions regarding my living arrangement surfaced. Grace and I had yet to discuss the rent, and I suspected she'd require more than I could afford. If God didn't intervene, I'd have no choice but to move back to Florida. I needed *rent-free*. Although free would be impossible, I secretly squeaked out the whim to God.

Was God shutting the doors here in Georgia? I didn't know. But I did know that my heart, soul and body were spent. What energy my heartache hadn't sapped, the room of first graders had. As much as I loved my students and longed to see my marriage restored, leaving town sounded sweeter with each tick of the clock.

Exhausted, I whispered, *"God, I don't care what you choose."* I didn't. *"Just make it obvious . . . please."*

One day after school, Grace called to discuss her rental price for the guest room. Our brief conversation made it clear. Even with the staff's love-gift each month I couldn't cover Grace's requested fee.

I hung up with a resolve. *He had made it obvious. Praise God.*

I didn't know how all this would turn out with JP, but the thought of going home was a relief. No more dependence on friends to help with the bills, no more exhausting days in class. I'd quietly disappear to my parents' home like a character being written out of a novel.

I walked back to my empty classroom. The stark overhead lights were off, but the sunlight from the room's windows filled the space with a soothing glow. The peace and quiet in the room matched my sentiment.

I had done my best. I had not quit. God was leading me elsewhere. That clarity gave me strength and determination to wrap up this season of my life as quickly as possible. No reason to drag it out. Plus, I had nowhere to sleep after tomorrow.

I wanted to speak with my principal, Maryellen. But on this particular day her administrative duties sent her out of the office. I'd have to wait until tomorrow to tell her I'd be leaving.

At least I could resign my nanny job today.

Several months earlier, to help make ends meet, I had picked up a part-time job watching a doctor's three children. Dr. Goldstein treated me well. Her children's care was of utmost importance to her and she deserved to know as soon as possible so she could find a suitable replacement.

As I gathered up my things to head to the Goldsteins, my friend Liz Anne appeared in the doorway, jarring me from my trance of resolve. She had news.

An older couple in their church lived in a large home on several acres of land with a pool, a barn and even a gardener.

Fancy.

Then she said, "I shared your story. I think they'll let you live with them, and I wouldn't be surprised if they let you stay with them for free."

Had she been listening to my prayer? I hadn't told anyone I'd asked God for that.

It sounded too good to be true. I told her I appreciated it, but I'd need to know by tomorrow. I intended on sharing my exit plan with the Goldsteins this afternoon and Maryellen tomorrow.

She said okay, and I went to my nanny job.

A note from Dr. Goldstein met me on the kitchen counter explaining that a friend would be picking up the kids at 5:30, and then I'd be free to go. Normally, I'd welcome a message like that, but today it perturbed me. I wanted to get this whole resigning thing behind me, and now I'd have to wait until . . .

Then it hit me.

Maryellen never missed work. Dr. Goldstein rarely sent me home early. Had God blocked me from resigning today? *God, You want me to stay? Realistically, I can only afford free, but what kind of people would allow a stranger to live with them . . . for free?*

My phone rang. It was Liz Anne.

"The Kellys said yes, and they have no intention of charging you." She read my mind. "And Rebecca, don't worry about the free thing. Trust me. They don't need your money."

I'd never seen or heard of these people before today, yet I barely questioned the opportunity. God had orchestrated the details so clearly that I said yes immediately.

⌒⌒

Of course, my first order of business entailed spying on the house. Though I didn't have a cell phone with GPS, I thought I could find the address. But the further I drove, the more lost I felt.

With every mile, another question hopped in the car with me. *What was I thinking moving into a home with people I've never seen before? JP, you're a jerk for putting me in this position, doggone it. Forget it. This is a ridiculous plan.* I spotted a stop sign up ahead. I decided when I reached that marker I would give up the search.

As I slowed for the stop, a strong impression flooded my heart. *What if it's just one street away? What if JP is close to repentance? You might be giving up with a miracle right around the corner.*

Give up or press on?

That's the trouble with uncharted waters. No one knows what's around the bend. *It could be just one street away. Or I could be miles off track and JP's heart as hard as granite.* I didn't know. I only knew that my spirit shouted louder to move forward than it did to retreat.

I traveled onward. To my great relief, the very next street was Steeple Bridge Road. *Left or right?* Guessing, I turned left.

I slowed my pace to scan for an address, but a car emerged right on my tail. I jetted into a subdivision entrance to let the car pass. Instead of passing, the car pulled into the driveway across the street—the driveway that matched the address I held in my hand.

The car brake lights lit up like a searchlight hunting a suspect. My heart jumped into my throat. *I am about to be caught red-handed for spying. Not exactly the first impression I wanted to make.*

I froze in my seat, willing myself invisible. The door opened, and an older gentleman stepped out. I held my breath. That must be Mr. Kelly, the owner of the house.

It felt like a huge arrow pointed at my car with a glowing

neon sign saying, "Hey mister. See this car and this crazy lady? She's the one you said could live with you. Yes, her. The one scoping out the joint!"

Thankfully, he headed toward the mailbox instead of towards me. I scrunched down in the seat as the man turned back to his car.

The brake lights released, and the car moved down the driveway. My heart settled and I focused my attention on the view before me. The landscaped entrance drew my eye down the gentle winding drive. At the end of the driveway, amid massive trees and a lush green yard, I caught glimpses of my new home. It peaked out gently among the foliage as if to say, "Welcome, Rebecca!" Peace resonated from the place, like the kind you feel while sinking into your favorite chair.

I'm so glad I didn't turn around one street too early.

⤔

WHAT I GAINED: God knows I want His will to be done, and He can spare me from making a wrong choice.

8

THE BEDSPREAD

It was a dark and stormy night.

Really, it was.

The bitter January sleet accompanied me as I gathered my things from Grace's house. The Kellys were hosting out-of-town guests, which pushed back move-in day to Sunday. That meant I had nowhere to live for the next four days. Never did I expect to be someone without an address. Although I had the promise of a place to stay, the reality that I didn't belong anywhere magnified my sense of vulnerability. I struck out to find the cheapest motel possible in a relatively safe part of town.

Thankfully, I found an affordable room where I could stay until I moved in with the people I had never met. *Moving into a home I have never seen inside with people I have never even spoken to? What am I doing?*

That's what I should have been thinking, but the thought

barely crossed my mind. God had moved mountains to get me to this point. I just knew His plan ended with a saved marriage and a testimony of restoration to shout from the rooftops.

At the hotel, I looked like any other customer, but I felt like a fluffy rabbit at a hungry fox convention with someone announcing, "Attention criminals. This scatterbrained lady is all by herself without a soul in sight to help her. She's an easy target because, *listen to this*, her husband doesn't have a clue where she is, nor does he care!" I fought the urge to run and hide behind every pole between my car and the motel room door like they do in the police movies.

Once inside, I exhaled for the first time in days. The tension of being an unwanted guest at Grace's house had taken its toll. My body felt like it weighed a thousand pounds, and I couldn't keep my eyelids open any longer. Knowing I wasn't intruding into someone else's space, I collapsed into a much-needed slumber.

My mom called that night. She'd be coming to stay with me until I had an address to call home. I told her I'd be fine, but she insisted. She couldn't come until the weekend, and that worked out fine in my book. Being holed up in a secluded room to sleep sounded perfect.

During my waking moments, I poured out my heart to God. With a little space to breathe, my thoughts pelted JP for putting me in this exposed position. But even in my anger, I missed him something terrible.

If only he would hold me and beg me to forgive him. I'd shout, "Yes!" before he could even finish the sentence. I longed to hear him tell me he'd do whatever it took to restore our relationship. But in our current state, that seemed a far-fetched fantasy.

On the other hand, I also knew that with God nothing was impossible. Restoring our marriage would take a heavy-duty commitment to God. I wasn't denying that. But I also knew that if JP were willing, God could make us whole again.

❡

Mom arrived. As the clock ticked closer to Sunday's move-in time, I felt my courage evaporating. It took all my strength to keep polite conversation going.

Fortunately, one of those conversations preoccupied me most of the weekend.

I love creative ideas. On Saturday morning I discovered a simple way to make a bed (yes, I know I was in a hotel room, but my mom always taught us to make our bed). I pulled my bedspread up about two feet past the headboard and folded it down to place my pillows on the folded part. I noticed the fabric was the same on the topside of the comforter as on the underside. So, I just slid the pillows under the folded part of the cover. *What a great idea.*

"Mom, look at this cool invention." I demonstrated the new discovery.

"When you were little, I made a sewing pattern just like that." She paused. "You're not going to believe this. I *just* dreamed about that bedspread last night."

My mom blew off the coincidence. I hung on like a

Doberman with a juicy bone. "I can't believe you dreamed about it last night after all these years. Mom, you've got to market this!"

I pounded her with the idea, relieved for anything hopeful that diverted attention away from my bizarre new world.

❦

Despite the valiant effort to be positive, by Sunday morning, my bravery levels were bankrupt. Getting ready for church, I forced my depression to hum and chat and whatever else carefree people do. But the more I thought about my situation, the faster bullets of doubt shot at my heart.

If I hoped to stick this out, I needed some reassurance. I confessed my charade to my mom, and we dropped to our knees. We asked God for a clear, unmistakable answer.

After we said amen, a vivid picture of the first day I struck out to find the Kellys' house came to mind. *I almost quit one street too early. What if I'm only "one street away" from a new marriage with JP? If I gave up one day or month too soon, I'd regret it my entire life.*

In my spirit, I knew the answer: move forward with the plan. My mom concurred. Later, we discovered how intensely we both fought the desire to run away and never look back.

❦

During church, life felt far away and out of reach. I forced myself to keep moving forward.

The sermon, however, grabbed my attention like a splash of color on a black and white photo. My pastor shared a story of a man who'd spent his last dime traveling the world in search of diamonds. Eventually, with his bank account empty, he sold his land to make ends meet.

The new landowners discovered an added bonus to the property. Diamonds. Turns out the precious gems had been under the jewel hunter's feet the whole time.

The illustration encouraged me, "Look at what's right in front of you." God provided a way for me to stay in Georgia. I could either trust Him or take matters into my own hands and go the easy route. No one would've blamed me. The only problem with the latter plan was that I'd be without God. I did not want that. No way. I'd pursue His go-live-with-the-strangers plan.

⁓

Pulling into the Kellys' driveway, an unexplainable confidence welled up inside me. I knocked on the front door.

No answer. *What if they're not home? What if they chickened out and hoped that if no one answered the door, then I'd just go away?*

I knocked again, a little louder this time.

No answer. My heart beat faster. *What am I supposed to do? Bang on the door like a crazed idiot, begging someone to take me?*

Giving up, my mom and I started walking back to the car when we heard a cheery, "Hello!"

From the garage side of the house, out walked a lady. She embraced us in a hug that somehow made me feel as if I'd known her my whole life and why in the world had I waited so long to come live with them?

"Hi, I'm Bobbie Kelly. You must be Rebecca. And you must be Rebecca's mom."

Like a robot, I answered, "Hi. I'm Rebecca, the girl who's supposed to live with you." It was all I could think to say.

As Mrs. Kelly led us through the house, I felt instantly

connected. If I had decorated this home, I would've chosen many of the same colors and furnishings. Feeling at home in my space was mega-important to me. This was no accident. My heart blurted out, *"God. I never thought of the décor of the home. You are so kind!"*

I may have missed this detail of God's thoughtfulness had it not been for the contrast of the home where I nannied. Its stark design clashed with my taste and reminded me that I was a visitor. But this home felt just like . . . home.

As we proceeded through several bedrooms and various living spaces, Mrs. Kelly directed us up the stairs to see my room. The top of the stairway had a small landing with two doors.

Mrs. Kelly said the door to the left would be my space. The other suite belonged to their daughter Stephanie who was away at college. The upstairs consisted of only two suites. *Incredible.* After several years of marriage, the thought of bunking up with others set my nerves on edge. But miraculously, God had arranged a place for me to be alone, yet not alone. His forethought and attention to detail awed me. I couldn't soak it in fast enough.

When we entered the suite that would be mine, my feet sank into plush cream-colored carpet, and the pale-yellow walls wrapped around me like a cloak of warm sunshine. We walked down a tastefully decorated hall with slanted walls until the room opened up to a large space complete with an antique bed and dresser, a quaint nightstand, a yummy yellow chair and the most adorable armoire I'd ever seen.

The bathroom opened to the left of the bed with gold fixtures, a skylight and soothing monochromatic yellow wallpaper with a classic raised motif. All of it, of course, matched the rest of the room perfectly. The bedspread, colored a bit darker than the walls, had bits of raspberry, pink and green in the scene depicted. My color palette to a T! The whole space felt oddly familiar.

When we finished the tour of the house—three floors, six bedrooms and numerous other spaces—we went to the family room to chat. Mrs. Kelly had never met my mother or me before, yet she seemed to care about me as if she was my dear aunt or close family friend.

As we sat down to talk, my frazzled appearance embarrassed me. No amount of makeup could cover my sadness. Dark circles framed my puffy tear-weary eyes and my hair lay wilted and lifeless. Twenty pounds ago, my clothes had fit. Now they bagged on my sunken body.

Up until this point, I rarely allowed others or even myself an honest look at my vulnerable, raw side. I thought it glorified God. Like I needed to protect His reputation and not allow my true feelings to manifest. Somewhere along the line, pride mingled in as well. As I traveled deeper down this path of desperation, God tenderly began to chisel away my carefully crafted façade of perfection. In my current survival mode, I'd been forced to reveal to others that "perfect Rebecca" wasn't so perfect after all.

Mrs. Kelly listened to a brief synopsis of my situation, taking in the information and intuitively filling in the gaps as if she had known the story all along. She didn't call me crazy for wanting my husband back. She didn't encourage me to put it all behind me and move on. Most importantly, she didn't make light of the fact that I believed God could work a miracle in our lives. In fact, she cheered my pursuit.

When we finished our conversation, the three of us prayed together. Peace rushed into my mom's expression as if a huge burden had been lifted. I felt it too.

My mom and I needed to retrieve our belongings from the hotel. Then my mom would drive back to Florida and I'd return to the Kellys'.

We had barely closed the car doors when my mom blurted out, "Rebecca. Did you see that bedspread?"

We had just seen six different bedspreads. They were all beautiful. I didn't understand her urgent tone. "Which bedspread?"

She was flabbergasted. "You mean you didn't see it?"

A bit flabbergasted at her flabergastedness I said, "Mom I don't have a clue what you mean."

"The bedspread in that yellow room was made exactly like the one I dreamed about the other night, and the one you've been babbling about for the last 24 hours. I thought for sure you noticed it too."

That sounded too bizarre to me. "Mom, are you sure? I don't remember it like that." *Seems like I would have noticed something so bizarre. With six different bedrooms in the house, the one they reserve for me has a unique bedspread exactly like the one my mom and I have been discussing for the past several hours?*

Back at the hotel, we said our goodbyes. But it wasn't sad. If she was upset, she didn't show it. (I found out later she cried the whole way home.) I could hardly wait to return to my new residence.

As I rounded the curve and caught sight of the Kellys' property, my eyes twinkled in awe at what God had done. I couldn't believe this beautiful place would be my home. My first thought was, "Oh, I can't wait till JP sees this!"

Logic said I should be furious and never want to speak to him again. After all, his ditch-and-run was the whole reason I landed here in the first place. Yet I *did* want to be with him, more than anything. I would have followed him anywhere if he'd reconcile.

Today, he felt miles away. But someday we'd be together again. Someday I'd show him this place. He'd be as impressed as I imagined him to be. He will be so grateful to the Kellys for taking care of his little wife. In the end, I'll have my husband back, and we will have gained life-long friends. I felt sure of it.

❧

Back at the Kellys' house, checking out the bedspread was first on my to-do list.

As I entered the large room, my mouth hung open like a dental patient with too much Novocain. There on the bed lay the unique bedspread just as my mom had said. I wish I could've been up near God, watching my expression. My eyes sparkled, and the circular shape of my mouth gradually formed into the curve of a smile. The kind of smile that looks up to God and says, "Oh my Father, I. Have. No. Words."

It wasn't until later that night that I realized why the space felt so familiar. It was shaped exactly like my childhood bedroom—the room where I met God for myself, where His word came alive to me. Oh, how I loved that room. Oh, how I loved this one.

Without a doubt, only God could have orchestrated these details. He had gone before me and lovingly prepared a space with me in mind. I could scarcely take it in. My heart swelled in awe of my Heavenly Father's tender care.

What I would have missed if I'd turned around one street too early.

❧

WHAT I GAINED: Don't quit when God is leading, no matter how bizarre or bleak the situation. It's in those moments that His display of power is beyond imagination.

9

MIRROR, MIRROR, ON THE WALL . . . (I *DO* HAVE ISSUES AFTER ALL)

Not all loss is bad.

After moving in with the Kellys, life became unfussy. With only enough clothes to get me through a week, choices were simple. Why would I want more than three t-shirts ever again? One to wear, one to sleep in and one to wash. Things that used to be important just didn't matter anymore, and I discovered the glorious unencumbered freedom of less stuff.

Nope, not all loss is bad.

While my outward routine stabilized, some profound soul work began percolating on the inside—something God began brewing during my two and half years teaching at Crestview Christian School. They hired me as a teacher, but I felt more like a privileged student.

The compassion bubbling from this community of people surpassed any I'd ever experienced. Being treated as a person with value—and not some machine to be used up and shoved in the corner when someone better came along—awakened a part of me I didn't know existed.

Crestview didn't love me because of what I might add to the organization, but rather because God created me in His image. Maryellen constantly stressed God's deep delight in us. My "try harder" soul stirred at the possibility of God delighting in me. The more I experienced God's grace and love dripping from her and the rest of the community, the more I realized I was missing something. I craved what they possessed. *But what was it?*

∽⚬∾

In my heart of hearts, I believed this debacle with JP would lead to a storybook ending. The optimism existed in part because JP said from the beginning he'd be willing to go to counseling. Maryellen's friend Scott, from Grace Ministries International (GMI), agreed to take us.

Even though I'd only spoken with him on the phone, I sensed he understood that churchy answers wouldn't help. Advice like, "you need to get your priorities right" or "you need to repent and surrender to God" hadn't benefitted JP one iota in the past. Focusing only on behaviors resulted in a deeper spiral of defeat. We needed to dig down to the root issues.

I just didn't know it would be my roots we'd be yanking at.

∽⚬∾

The counseling plan included joint sessions, along with JP and me meeting individually with Scott. When my turn came for private counseling, I poured out my heart. I explained I'd done my very best to be a good wife. Even though JP betrayed me, I'd be willing to do *anything* to save our marriage.

Then Scott asked me an odd question. "Are you willing to work on your issues?"

I wondered if he'd been listening to me at all. "I'm willing to do whatever I can to help JP and save our marriage."

"I realize that, but are you willing to look at your issues?"

I kind of giggled, as much out of shock as anything. I knew he counseled a lot of people, but I wanted to be sure he understood the situation. I told him point-blank, "I'm not the one with the problem. I have *no* regrets as to how I've treated JP. I love my husband with all my heart. And I love the Lord. JP is the one who's been unfaithful. Not me."

Once again in his kind yet firm way, he asked, "But are you willing to look at *your* issues?"

I sat stunned, and then repeated my previous statement.

After the *third* time (I'm quick like that), I realized he wasn't asking because he misunderstood the circumstances. He obviously recognized problems in me that needed to be examined. All my thoughts collided like a five-car pile-up.

I confessed, "I honestly don't know what you're talking about, but I do want help. And yes, I am *absolutely* willing to look at my own issues." I meant it.

❧

I had barely started to process Scott's question when it just so happened that—totally a God thing—within the next few days, our staff attended a teacher workshop.

The lecturer described students who'd do whatever they could to please the teacher, in hopes of gaining approval and love. My mind raced to different children who fit that narrative. They believed that if they followed all the rules or answered correctly the teacher would love them more. The nurturer in me ached at their misunderstanding. I pictured myself bent down to their eye-level, pleading with them to realize that I loved them no matter what they did or didn't do.

Suddenly, the scene changed, and I was one of the children struggling to get God to notice how well I behaved, how hard I tried. God bowed low to my level asking, "*Rebecca*, don't you see? You do the same thing as your students. But I don't love you because you do well. I love you because you're Mine!"

As a young girl, I accepted Jesus as my Savior. But I unknowingly equated God loving me with being a good girl. I couldn't comprehend that even if I did everything utterly wrong and failed Him every day, He still longed for me.

I'd heard it before, but this day the weight of God's love hit me with the force of an ocean wave. My heart pounded. I swiped at the teardrops spilling down my face. The deep emotion stirring in my chest threatened to rupture into crowd-stopping sobs right in the middle of the conference room. The session couldn't end fast enough.

At the break, I bolted into the restroom stall so my heart could burst in private. Growing up, I'd heard that if we ever grasped how much God loved us, we'd curl up in the fetal position and weep. That statement always shocked me. Now I understood.

Rocking uncontrollably back and forth, I folded up in a ball and cried. "*No, God. There must be something I can do to deserve Your love. I'll be really good . . .*" But even as the prayer left my lips, I knew the suggestion was ludicrous. I could never be good enough on my own.

On one hand, to think that God would love me in all my failure made my spirit soar, light and free. On the other hand, I couldn't give up my pride and receive His love with nothing to offer back.

I tried to bargain again. *"Something. Please God. I'll work really hard . . . "* That was ridiculous. I could never work hard enough to deserve even a drop of what He'd done for me.

Every time I made a plea, I envisioned Him with a gleam in His eye, His voice steady and sure. "No, honey. There's nothing you can do. It's already done."

I pictured Him cupping my face in His palms. "I love you so much." Then His sweet smile fell on me as He said with a slight chuckle, "I adore you!"

Finally, I could resist Him no longer. I released my pride—pride that believed I could be good enough to *deserve* His favor. And I fell into His ocean of unconditional love and delight.

⌒⌒

It took several days before I could articulate the freedom God showed me that day. Mere words are still inadequate to describe it. I wondered how I could've loved God and considered Him my best friend for almost thirty years and yet be so ignorant of my pride in contrast to His true nature.

Obviously, I had much to learn.

⌒⌒

As God would have it, within the next few weeks JP and I were able to schedule a joint session onto Scott's calendar. He just had one stipulation. We needed to attend the three-day Grace Ministries International *Christ Is Life* workshop. I agreed instantly. JP's consent surprised me. Then it thrilled me. This could be a turning point. I hoped it proved further evidence of my storybook-ending theory.

As the weekend arrived, my mind pinged like a wild

pinball from one emotion to another. What if JP sat unaffected? In the past few months, I noticed something unsettling about his eyes. They were vacant. Not angry, not sad. Not even dead. Just empty. Like cold, round marbles. It scared me. The JP I married had vanished. I had no idea when or why he left. And I had no idea where he was or if he was ever coming back. The desperate part of me could barely concentrate on the speaker's message as I tried to decipher JP's reaction to what he heard.

Another part of me felt like a child headed to Disney World. I couldn't wait to be near JP for the whole weekend. The packed room forced us to squeeze together. With his shoulder touching mine, my body instantly relaxed, and a familiar warmth spread itself all over my insides. Was he feeling it too?

The full room, the closeness to JP and the anticipation of his response all fought for my attention.

In the end, JP made it through two-night sessions, but on the last day he ducked out with a flimsy excuse. My heart sputtered. Had anything he heard pricked his heart? I didn't know.

Somehow, in the midst of these distractions, the Spirit of God began opening my eyes to the warped thought-patterns and behaviors I'd developed.

My current belief system required me to look and act faultless because faultless was the rule. I was good at following rules because that gave me something I desperately craved—acceptance. I related to a quote from *Grace for the Good Girl*: "I perform because I don't know how not to. When bad girls perform to get their needs met, they get in trouble. When good girls perform to get the same needs met, they get praise."[1]

Even as a child, I had a burning desire to proclaim God's

goodness to the world. People praised my "heart for God." But somewhere along the line, the waters muddied, and I confused man's praise with God's delight in me. Affirmation became a rush I craved. Needed. No praise from man, no nod of approval from God.

My relational style took a big hit from this belief. I developed protective strategies to ensure I remained approved by others. I had to in order to be loved by God. I lived calculated. Avoided risk. And anytime I felt vulnerable, I withdrew from people and situations to retain a sense of control over the outcome.

If someone appeared dissatisfied or angry, I saw it as God being upset with me, thereby making it my duty to resolve the conflict regardless of the consequences it dumped on me. But when problems resolved because of me, it validated my worth. Maybe that's why it fed my inner person to "rescue" others.

Accepting a compliment or a gift troubled me, too. On my twenty-fifth birthday I agreed to host a birthday bash for JP and me, since our birthdays were within days of each other. Excitement and dread bantered inside my head like a good cop/bad cop routine. Even though I longed to be celebrated, I couldn't enjoy it. My pride wouldn't allow me to receive unless I thought I earned it or could pay it back. And this time, it was just too much to repay.

Now I understood why.

With these flaws in my flesh exposed, a whole cavern of yuck came to light. I remembered times I took someone a meal when they were sick. If I had done it to get a "good Christian credit," instead out of an overflow of love, then the joke was on me. God saw right through those motives. Memory after memory came flooding back of times I'd used people to beef up my image instead of loving them like

Christ loved me.

Until the *Christ is Life* workshop, I never realized how self-absorbed and wrong I'd been.

In the past, my default solution for failure was to beat myself up and vow to do better next time—again, trusting in myself to earn God's smile. When I did better, it was a good day. When I didn't, it was bad. Hence the rollercoaster of defeat and victory continued, and it was exhausting.

I needed a new normal.

God had one for me, but it required something—a willingness to be broken, to embrace my inability and give up my power (or my *perception* of power) and control. That meant humbling myself. Ouch. It meant releasing my right to be right, to be loved, to have a good reputation, to be the favorite, to have pleasant circumstances.

It felt scary and impossible . . . until I realized that Christ embraced brokenness for me. On the cross, He released His right to be protected, to be validated, to be loved and respected. And unlike me, the perfect Son of God *did* have the right to those things. He could've smitten every last one of His accusers with a word.

But He didn't.

He chose brokenness, laid down His privilege and hung on that cross, humiliated.

And He did it for me.

Next to His humility, my audacity disgusted me. The shame I felt from a lifetime of manipulating and propping myself up brought me to my knees. The only offering in my hands was my selfish pride. But if I'd let it go, I could walk in the righteousness I'd received as a young girl.

At that moment, I chose brokenness.

Suddenly, the pressure to guard the persona of perfection fell away, and the relief felt like trading an outfit two sizes too small for the most comfortable pajamas in the world. I could be vulnerable and authentic because I was righteous. Not because I was good but because God was. Now I could love from a heart focused on the dear ones around me rather than the impression I may or may not be making on them.

I don't know exactly when or how I began to change, but the mask I used to don started peeling away. As a result of being honest about my struggles, others started trusting me with their painful and sometimes shameful pasts.

My new perspective also uncovered the ways people (myself included) put their identity in what they wore, how they looked or performed in a given situation. The more I observed these coping mechanisms, the more obvious and ridiculous they appeared.

It didn't mean I couldn't enjoy wearing a nice outfit or being successful, as long as my participation was in a celebration of who God made me to be and not for the protection of my "image."

ᕙᕙᕤ

Grasping a concept doesn't mean you automatically understand how to apply it. It often takes time to see how the principles play out in real life. It's like getting your hair done by your stylist. You love it, but now you've got to go home and figure out how to do it yourself.

Somehow, I needed to practice allowing God's love to be enough regardless of how others viewed me. And God had the perfect classroom. He placed me in the choir of a large mega-church.

So much of my life had been in the spotlight, but not here. My face blended into the crowd—which might have been the best thing that ever happened to me. Those months of anonymity helped me shed the need for another's approval in order to feel God's smile on me.

I fought it though. It felt as uncomfortable as a right-handed person swinging a golf club left-handed. I longed to prove my worth to my new church family. But God wanted to teach me a vital lesson much more than He needed my measly contribution.

As I tried to grasp this new way of relating to myself, others and God, I still struggled deeply with the rejection of my husband, the person I loved more than anyone else in the world. I'd given my absolute best, yet it wasn't enough.

I kept praying for restoration. But I questioned. *God, how do I live in both faith and reality? The reality is JP may never come back to You or me. But doesn't faith say the opposite? Maybe I'm doing something wrong.*

One night the struggle sucked all logic out of me. The more I tried to figure it out, the more tangled my thoughts became. *Maybe I needed to pray more. Maybe I have a strange thing about me. Or maybe JP has just gone off the deep end.*

At this stage in the game, I believed our relationship could go either way. What could I do to bring him home to us? The pressure to make the right choices squeezed like a boa constrictor.

Then my brother Reed called.

He wanted me to know that he had called JP. I appreciated his willingness to risk confrontation in hopes of helping us. After speaking with JP, Reed concurred that our marriage had a fifty-fifty chance of survival.

I blurted out, "I don't know what I'm supposed to do. The more I try to figure it out the more confused I get. I don't know the balance between tough love and grace. I'm so afraid I'll make the wrong move or say the wrong thing!"

I felt like I'd go crazy trying to work this out in my mind. I couldn't bear the thought of disappointing God or making a mistake that would ruin a chance to reconcile.

Reed picked up on my frenzy. "Beck, think about God, as if he were like Dad. What would Dad do right now if he were listening to you?"

I knew right away. Without missing a beat, I said, "He would hold me tight and say, 'Daddy loves you, honey.'"

I knew my dad loved me whether I had been a good girl or not. My brother reminded me that God was no different. Tears flowed, bringing with them a deep inward cleansing. I was so tired of struggling to hold it all together, trying to be good enough or right enough for my husband to come back. That night I crumbled into my Father's arms, arms that had been aching for me to find refuge in Him.

⌒⌒

When I was a little girl, I experienced life-threating illnesses. My dad would say in a voice that was more thinking out loud than speaking, "I wish I could be sick instead of you."

I didn't understand the magnitude of that statement then. I thought all dads said stuff like that because they had to. But as I matured, I realized he really did wish he could take my place.

It dawned on me. That was exactly what Christ did for me on the cross. He became sick—sin-sick—so I could be whole. My dad's example of unconditional love nurtured my budding new belief system. Like my dad, God loved me not because of what I could do, but He loved me even when I was frail and useless.

I don't claim that God caused all this to happen so He could reveal Himself to me (although, that is possible). But I do claim that God will not waste one moment of darkness in our lives. Ultimately, He can use our loss to give us a clearer understanding of Himself.

He said in Isaiah 45:3 that He will give us "the treasures of darkness." Much to the Enemy's chagrin, God revealed delights of His true self in those deep caverns.

I nearly missed it. I became so engrossed in JP's problem that I almost rejected the thought that God wanted to scrape the gunk out of *my* heart. But now I could walk free from the burden of performing for His love.

In the end, that treasure far outweighed the darkness required for me to find it.

No, not all loss is bad.

❦

WHAT I GAINED: In the darkness, God revealed rich treasures about Himself I would not have discovered in comfort and ease.

10

THE RIGHT TO WRONG BACK

Deep down, I knew if I could have been Betty Crocker, Miss America and Joanna Gaines all rolled up into one terrific package, JP and I would still be in the same miserable boat. His problem went far beyond our relationship. Our marriage was simply reaping the consequences of a life grasping for something to gratify the hole in his heart.

But that's what made it so aggravating. I *knew* God had the answer. If JP would accept the things we were learning about God at Grace Ministries, he would understand that all these efforts to satisfy his soul were worthless. God could and would heal him . . . and us.

While he rarely contacted me, the few times he did convinced me to hold out hope for our reconciliation. I missed JP something terrible. But in an effort to invoke tough love, I rarely initiated communication with him. Barely a moment passed without him trampling through my thoughts. It took every ounce of willpower I had to refrain from seeking him out.

⌒⌒

I hadn't seen him in weeks. One day I needed something from our house, so I purposely picked a time I knew he'd be home to fetch my item. I wanted to respect his privacy, so I called to warn him I'd be by at a specific time. He said that would be fine. No big deal.

Not really. It was a big deal to me. I couldn't wait to see him.

On the outside, I nonchalantly followed my Sunday routine. But on the inside, the moments got stuck in molasses as I waited for the clock to hit the appointed time. The prospect of seeing him made me happier than I wanted to admit.

I drove the twenty minutes to the house suppressing my urge to floor it through all the red lights. I didn't expect to stay long. I had no visions of life-changing conversation or instant relational renewal. I just wanted to see him. I wouldn't admit this out loud, but maybe if he saw me, he'd remember all the good times.

Wearing my favorite dress and freshly applied lipstick, I pulled into the driveway.

I didn't even notice Old Blue missing from its parking spot. When I reached the front steps, however, I did see a note on the door.

Sorry, I missed you. I had to run out.

"What? Sorry, I missed you!" I huffed out loud. The realization that he purposely left to avoid contact with me launched an atomic bomb that exploded in my soul.

He figured out my plan. That left him to devise a plan of his own—to be long gone by the time I got there.

All the way back to my car hurt and humiliation scoffed in my ear. But before I opened the door, anger and pride snuck up beside me and urged me to shove my shame into the gravel. I agreed wholeheartedly. "Well, I won't be humiliated. Not this time."

Sitting in the driveway, I called the house phone knowing I could leave a message. As the answering machine kicked in, and without even batting an eye, I nonchalantly said, "Hey JP. Just wanted you to know I can't make it by today. Didn't want you to wonder what was up."

I lied.

Boldface lied as if I fibbed every day. I was sick of being duped. I would outsmart him this time. After everything he'd put me through, he didn't deserve the truth anyway.

There. I'd finally one-upped him. The retaliation felt *great* . . . for a brief moment. Extremely brief.

After the initial rush of gratification, the truth that he intentionally left to elude me shattered any victorious thoughts I'd felt.

Truth be told, through our bits of counseling and conference attendance, I sensed the gulf between us enlarging. He called less often, and his excuses were as thin as a slight freeze on a Minnesota pond. Apparently, I wasn't the only one noticing the increasing distance. Those who'd been rooting for us stopped offering possible justifications for JP. Instead, I sensed they were biting their tongue from saying something.

My mom had long since encouraged me to pack up my things and come home. Others close to me began acting funny, like they understood something I was still too blind to see. Their eyes filled with fresh pity when I walked in a room, like I was someone who just stood up to speak, unaware of the toilet paper hanging down her backside.

Eventually, I started suspecting a change in our counselor's perspective toward JP too. While he never discussed anything that JP shared with him during his sessions, I got the impression that things weren't looking good for the little wifey.

I still wasn't convinced.

Apparently, I suffered from what is commonly defined as defensive hope. According to Dr. Larry Crab and Dr. John Townsend in their book *Safe People*, defensive hope is "hope that protects us against grief and sadness. Sometimes simply hoping a person will change keeps us from the pain that we need to face. Humans are incredible optimists when it comes to destructive relationships. For some reason we think that a person who is hurtful, irresponsible or out of control, abusive, or dishonest is going to change if we just love them correctly or more or enough." (Oh, super guilty of that!)

"In short, we have hope, but it is a hope that disappoints. In this scenario we use hope to defend ourselves against facing the truth about someone we love. We don't want to go through the sadness of realizing that they probably are not going to change. We don't want to accept the reality about who they are. So, we hope." [1]

This incident at the house cracked open a door of realization for me. JP's absence was no coincidence. Reality wasn't just knocking anymore; it flat-out leveled my heart like a wrecking ball. I couldn't just prop it back up or excuse it away this time.

But I was confused. As a Christian, I believed as long as JP had breath, God could change his heart. That belief had allowed me to shut my eyes to a ton of red flags in the name of faith. I wasn't ready to give up all hope yet, but finally the facts started taking root. Even after months of separation, this was the first time I allowed myself to move past the shock and entertain the idea that maybe his heart had moved on from mine . . . forever

I drove from the empty house to a nearby parking lot and sobbed. Loud. And hard. And sometimes in eerie silence.

～○～

I don't know how long I stayed in that parking lot.

When I finally made it back to the Kellys' house, I realized I had another problem. In the past, I'd always had the Lord. Regardless of how painful or difficult the experience, I could collapse into His arms and rest in His promises to take all things and work them together for good.[2]

But when I lied on the voicemail, I deliberately told God, "I believe I'll handle this my own way!" I blew off the verse about speaking truth[3] and the one that explicitly says, "Vengeance is mine."[4] I was tired of waiting on His plan to pay off.

I tried to excuse it away, like it was no big deal. No one had been put out or harmed in the act. Compared to the downright violations of sacred covenant JP had committed, this seemed like a tiny speck of dirt in the river of purity. I wanted to square my shoulders and puff out my chest to convince myself I had every right to act the way I did. In light of the circumstances—*ahem*—I wasn't guilty of anything.

But regardless of how many times JP had lied to me, it couldn't justify my untruthfulness to him. I had taken matters into my own hands and left God out. But leaving God out of my life was the last thing I wanted.

I admitted to God that instead of letting Him take care of me, I had decided to defend myself. I confessed it to Him as sin. But even after acknowledging my wrong before God, I knew I wasn't finished.

True repentance required one more step.

If I could've made a deal in which I promised to humiliate myself on stage in front of a crowd, it would have seemed a better trade than doing what I knew I needed to do—confess my wrong to JP.

I had a list of reasons why not to admit to JP what I'd done. First of all, he would think I was stupid for apologizing about such a seemingly insignificant fib, especially after all the lies he'd told me through the years. But most of all, I'd have to admit he hurt me. I dreaded that.

I tried again to convince myself that my one little lie was insignificant compared to his life-shattering ones. I almost persuaded myself of some fake right that allowed me to respond any way I pleased—that God would turn His head and ignore my wrong. But I couldn't escape the truth that God doesn't compare me to JP.

His wrongs toward me didn't excuse my sin.

I had to ask myself, "Did I outright lie?"

Yes, I did.

I could argue all I wanted, but right is still right. This wasn't about being wrong in JP's eyes. This was about being right in *God's* eyes. Being reminded again that my husband didn't want me wore my edges raw, but nothing compared to the loneliness of separating myself from God. My pride before JP wasn't worth sacrificing my intimacy with the Lord. The desire to be right with Him granted me the courage to face my sin.

I called JP later that night. I hoped to leave a message again, but after a couple rings he answered. My stomach knotted when I heard his voice on the other end. I figured it best not to think and plow ahead with the confession.

I blurted out that I'd lied to him today on his voicemail. I did in fact come over, and when I saw the note I was hurt. I told him, "I didn't want you to know I cared, so I called you and left the message." I laid it out there, no holding back or dipping the truth in chocolate.

JP's reaction shocked me. He didn't ridicule me or make

light of the situation as I suspected he would. Rather, he thanked me for calling, and by his tone I accepted it as sincere, an unexpected bonus. Even if JP hadn't responded favorably, the bottom-line for me was that I was back under God's authority and protection. Nothing could replace that blessed relief and peace.

I'm not sure what I expected to feel when I'd followed through on my end of the responsibility, but when I hung up the phone, I discovered a new kind of free. The heavy cloud following me all afternoon had suddenly dissipated. No more five-thousand-pound weight to carry through the night. Regardless of the exhaustion from grieving the rejection, my clean conscience lightened my heart.

By requiring me to repent, my Heavenly Father wasn't trying to be harsh to me. He experienced my pain along with me. It's never okay with Him when His children are mistreated, shamed or abandoned. But even then, it's not my right to wrong back.

I wish I'd rested in the Lord instead of being sucked into the trap of handling things my own way. I found myself acting the way the Israelites did when God warned them about trusting other nations for their deliverance.

In the story, God let His children know He delights in showing Himself strong on behalf of those who put their trust in Him.[5] But even after God repeatedly stepped in and saved their scrawny necks, they still gravitated to other countries to protect them and devised ways to meet their own needs.

In the past, I've clucked my tongue at the foolishness of this nation. And yet, I was guilty of the same gravitational draw. In the blink of an eye, I had embraced my own method and removed myself from His protection.

But even in my failure, God provided me a way back to Him. He promised in I John 1:9 "If we confess our sins he is faithful and just to forgive us our sin and cleanse us from all unrighteousness."

He cleansed me from *all* of it.

No amount of wealth or ease can compete with the deep joy of a restored relationship with Him. In the future, I would choose God's way. Thankfully, with a clear conscience before God and JP I could lay my head down . . . and sleep.

WHAT I GAINED: Regardless of the wrong done to me, it doesn't give me the right to wrong back.

11

THE BEAUTIFUL BOUQUET

I held the phone to my ear dumbfounded.

The insurance lady, however, saw it all quite clearly. My husband had stopped paying the car insurance, so the company dropped me six months ago.

"There must be a mistake." I couldn't fathom that JP would knowingly let me drive around without insurance.

The lady held her ground. The insurance company had called our house and mailed notifications, but no one responded. They had no choice but to cancel me.

"But I had no idea. I'll pick up the payments now that I am aware." It made perfect sense to my naïve mind. Surely, they could understand my difficult situation and take pity. My husband abandoned me, plain and simple. If I'd known, I would have done something.

I wasn't playing dumb. I *was* dumb. I didn't have a clue how insurance policies worked. "Please, is there any way to make an exception?"

No go.

Finally, the woman conceded to reinstating the policy for a one-time upfront fee of one thousand dollars in addition to my regular payment. Was that supposed to be good news? I couldn't decide. I barely had the money to pay my small phone bill, let alone a chunk of cash that amount.

It wouldn't have been so bad except Atlanta had just experienced one of its worst hailstorms in history. My car looked like it had been in a back-alley brawl with a baseball bat. Even if I paid the fee, the lady informed me, I hadn't had coverage during the time of the storm, so no, they wouldn't pay to fix the damages.

It sounds silly to be attached to a lifeless object, but that car had been my one constant through all the changes. I hated leaving the Camry in such a deplorable condition. Now everywhere we traveled, we'd *both* feel the pity of observant eyes. I felt embarrassed to be so obviously cast aside. My car's new dents and scars exposed the truth: my beloved had hung me out to dry.

Nope. I didn't have a plan for how to reinstate the insurance. In fact, it felt so out of reach, I barely mentioned it to God. I just closed my eyes in resignation and whispered, "God, what do I do? I need a ton of money. Please help."

My coworker, Donna, stopped me in the hallway a few days after the hailstorm. Donna and I both taught first grade. She wasn't flashy or pretentious. I loved that about her.

Although we didn't spend time together outside of work, I considered her one of my dearest friends.

Her mother had recently passed away leaving her a small inheritance. She said, "Rebecca, this morning when I was praying about what to do with the money, God told me to give you a thousand dollars." She made the statement as if she'd gotten a buy-one-get-one-free deal on pencil sharpeners and wanted to give the other one to me.

Did she find out about the insurance? I hadn't told anyone. The only person at school who knew was . . . well, God. *Could He have told her?*

I immediately rejected her offer. "Oh, no Donna. I can't accept your money!"

"I'm going to give it away to someone. It might as well be to you."

She had a point. I weighed the situation. Donna wasn't the type to make up some story about praying if it wasn't true. She said what she meant, and she meant what she said. Besides, I desperately needed precisely the amount she offered.

Finally, I agreed to accept her gift. But I had to ask, "Donna, did you know I need exactly one thousand dollars to be reinstated by my insurance company?" Her mouth gaped, then smiled. She had no idea.

❦

I never doubted God's power. I only doubted His power to work for *me*, but His constant provision began eroding that lie. God kept showing up and I was learning a valuable, multi-faceted lesson. He would indeed supply my physical needs.

In addition to the free housing and the cash my coworkers collected for me, extra resources appeared almost weekly from a variety of sources. One week, my brother's church sent a check from their benevolence fund. A friend offered to pay my way to a ladies' conference. I picked up added income cleaning the building when the school janitor needed time off, and the school asked me to administer the entrance exams, earning me a little supplementary cash each time a session took place. My nanny job needed me an extra day here and a little early there. And Dr. Goldstein paid well for the additional commitment. I picked up a few tutoring students, and the exact amount of money I needed for a passport "magically" appeared in my teacher mailbox. Our staff had been invited overseas to an invitation-only conference. After my life's upheaval, I assumed my attendance was out of the question, but the administration and staff assured me that God (through them) would provide.

Week after week, I watched God show Himself strong on my behalf. It wasn't conventional provision. The source changed continually, but I soon began resting in the fact that even though I couldn't figure it out, God would supply.

Learning to receive from others chiseled away at my pride. In its place, I discovered something poignantly wonderful about being desolate—utter dependence on my God. Over time, I realized it's okay to need help, and it's humbling and beautiful to accept the generous offer of another.

❧

As days moved to weeks, I grew to understand God wanted to provide for more than my *physical* needs. He intended to meet *all* my needs: the mental, emotional, social and spiritual needs as well.

Being an insulin-dependent diabetic and limited in what I can eat and drink, it's no secret to those close to me how much I relish the diet drink TAB. One year for my birthday, my class made me a cake that looked like a six-pack of TAB. Pinterest would have been proud.

But TAB is more than a sugar-free drink to me. God has used it as a secret sign between the two of us to remind me He sees me, and He knows just how to bless my socks off.

With a bit of change in my wallet and payday not until the end of the week, I hoped to manage financially a few more days.

On this particular day, our middle school held a bake sale for an upcoming trip. My student, Gabe, approached my desk. He gulped down his nervousness and feebly handed me a crumpled-up dollar bill. With big brown eyes staring straight into mine he said, "I want you to buy yourself a treat at the bake sale."

That dear boy. With his wrinkled bill I had just enough money to purchase a nice cold TAB. But more than Gabe's generosity, my heart swelled at God's desire to spoil me and indulge my whims.

❧

One day a friend asked me to babysit her kids. Instead of paying me, she bought me a darling pearl bracelet. I never would have bought myself such a frivolous treat. Staring at it, I thanked God continually for allowing me the beautiful luxury.

A few weeks later, I looked down. The bracelet was gone.

With so much loss in my life I couldn't spare the energy to care. I hopped on the emotional pendulum and turned cynical instead. I swung from thankful to resentful bitterness that God would give me the gift just to take it away. The fake pearls suddenly represented what it felt like He was doing in my life, toying with me like a schoolyard bully.

I tried to blow it off. "Yeah, whatever. I didn't care about it anyway. It's just a silly bracelet."

But I *did* care about it. I wanted the jewelry back, but I didn't have the courage to ask for it. All the unanswered prayers for my marriage came flooding back. My heart couldn't handle the disappointment of yet another rejected request. I knew God could snap His holy fingers and make life work . . . but He didn't.

One day, Dr. Goldstein needed me to arrive early to watch the children. But she'd asked me to enter the house through the front door this time instead of the garage.

Weary, yet thankful for the extra work, I trudged head down through the thick lawn to the front door. I remember thinking, "Hmm . . . in all these months, I've never used the front door."

Then I saw it—my lovely pearl bracelet lay sprawled in

the grassy carpet. *It must have fallen off playing soccer with Josh.* Somehow it managed to stay in the yard unharmed for several days. In the dense grass, I never would've noticed it had I not come directly upon it. My path just "happened" to cross it.

I wasn't going to die if I never found it, but He gave it back to me anyway. If God heard my silent cries for a bracelet, then He certainly heard the pleas for my husband. And God filled my emotional tank yet again.

I started claiming the promise of Philippians 4:19 not just for my physical needs but my social needs as well. God began adding people to fill these needs. Throughout the course of three years, he weaved loving people in and out of my life.

I'd head into choir and say, "Okay God, you promised to meet *all* my needs. I don't know where to sit." When I entered the room, I felt as unsure and conspicuous as a teenybopper walking in her first pair of high heels—every time. But every time, He provided someone to include me.

I needed a roommate for a once-in-a-lifetime choir tour. All the ladies I knew had already paired up. A woman I'd only said hello to offered several of us newbies a spot in her room. I didn't even know her name, but her thoughtful inclusion made a lasting impression on me. Once again God provided.

It became an unofficial Thursday routine for my friend Tonya to invite me to her home for dinner. JP and I had met her and her husband Phil at church a few years earlier, and we loved hanging out with them.

After I moved to the Kellys', Tonya was the only friend I had consistent contact with who knew both JP and me. So many aspects of my life had changed; in some ways it felt as though I'd never existed before this crisis. I needed someone who knew who I was and who JP was, someone who understood why I missed him because she and Phil did too.

Thursday nights used to be filled with JP's exciting basketball games. Up to this point in our lives, I hadn't missed a game. I grieved that I never got to say goodbye to the kids. *Do they know that I still root for them?* In the quiet evenings, this question haunted me most: *Is someone else taking my place as JP's number one fan?*

Having something planned on those nights softened the blows. Tonya's two little girls squealed with joy when I walked in the side door and my heart warmed. I read them books and played silly games. While Tonya and I puttered in the kitchen we solved all the world's problems as only girlfriends can do. Phil, being an insulin dependent diabetic, brought another level of connection and validation to me. They both understood the unique challenges a diabetic faces, especially during stressful life events.

Being in their home allowed me a few minutes of daily family life in a kick-off-your-shoes-and-help-clear-the-table sort of way. Tonya will never know how much those meals at her kitchen table meant to me.

Then there was Claire. She didn't know the word "safe" and took God at His word in a way I'd never witnessed. I drank in her spiritual wisdom and insight. Her single life frequently freed her up to grab a bite to eat or take in a movie. Often, we ended the evening praying together for God's direction and peace in our lives.

One time, Claire volunteered to pick me up from the airport after a few days in Florida. I was a wreck. I'd lost so much weight that my clothes sagged and the circles under my puffy eyes looked like baby storm clouds settling in for the long haul.

If I were picking up a friend from the airport, I'd make sure I arrived on time (although, I've even failed at that basic step). I'd greet them with a warm smile and a big hug. I'd tote their luggage and refuse to take any money for the parking garage. I'd ask if they'd like to get something to eat, and then I'd do the next logical thing—the whole reason I came in the first place—I'd take them home.

Not Claire.

Yes, she greeted me on time with a cheery smile and a welcome-home hug. But when we got in the car, she pulled out her cooler filled with TAB chilled to perfection, with slivers of ice chips that slipped down your throat when you swallowed. The beautiful weather screamed picnic, so she'd whipped up my favorite meal of fried chicken and mashed potatoes.

She drove to a lovely park nestled among huge color-

139

soaked trees. The sound of laughing children and a refreshing breeze danced around us as we chatted honestly. No need to guard my words with Claire. No explanation or sugarcoating required. "I'm looking older these days. My face looks burdened and weary. I know."

She didn't try to convince me otherwise or offer a fake response like, "Oh you don't look so worn out, Rebecca." She just listened and nodded.

Everyone should have a friend like Claire. I could count on her to tell me the brutal truth. She'd say things like, "Your flesh is used to being stroked, like a china doll that is admired. When a flaw is exposed you don't know how to handle it, so you hide."

Sometimes it shocked me, but it never hurt because I knew the bravery it took to confront. She spoke from a heart of love and I grew because of it.

౭ᴖ౨

Tracy was my soul mate and confidant. Our first day of teaching together we realized we were like matching socks plucked out of a pile of laundry and finally paired up. We'd both been cheerleaders and loved sports. Nurturing our students hit high on both our radars. We adored our husbands and desired our homes to be our number one priority. At times, I wondered if we shared the same heart.

We also shared a deep ache. We were both barren. Infertility's private pain knit our hearts together and we leap-frogged over the usual time it takes to link a heart with another. We were in the same boat. Since there was no way out, I thank God He let me be in it with Tracy.

Her husband's job transferred them to South Florida, but we stayed connected. She often called or wrote on the exact day I needed it. Tracy understood the deep love of a wife for her husband and didn't hold it against me or discourage me from desiring JP back.

I met Christy after JP and I were apart. She was a young wife, a new Christian and new to teaching. Although she had never met JP, she let me talk about him as if she did. For some reason that was important to me.

Originally, she sought me out as a mentor, but ended up being a great friend. Her husband's school and work schedule left her flying solo especially on the weekends. That fit perfectly with my sad sack of a schedule, and we ended up spending a ton of time together.

Christy loved adventure and knew how to have fun. Seeing life through her eyes helped me bite through the pain and gave me a new perspective.

Christy hadn't grown up in a Christian home. Now that she'd accepted Christ, she was like a baby bird hungry to know more of God. While she desired for me to teach her, she taught me. Her oblivion to religious rules allowed her to live free. She challenged my preconceived ideas about life and God and what was most important. She simply wanted to know God and see Him work in her life.

Mr. and Mrs. Kelly, my kindhearted hosts, wove me into their lives as if I belonged to them. They took me to dinner and included me in their family functions. I tagged along on work events and trips. While they rubbed shoulders with wealthy people, they remained warm and down to earth. I observed how to function in a world far beyond my experience. I had no idea how valuable that training would be in the days to come. I never dreamed how much I'd grow to love them.

Mr. Kelly loved to give. He faithfully made my lunch and stockpiled the fridge with TAB just like my dad used to do. He was a great conversationalist and we enjoyed philosophical discussions. His masculine perspective on life and his protectiveness helped ground me and make me feel safe.

Mrs. Kelly reminded me so much of my mom. She often came up to my room at night to check on me. She'd sit at the end of the bed as I unloaded a dump truck full of fears and hurt. She listened, no matter how convoluted my thoughts spilled out.

Heartache and trouble had shoved their way into her life as well. Her insights and perspectives repeatedly set me back on course. We usually ended up laughing somewhere in our conversation, and I'd take note. Even in the midst of all her trials, she could laugh. Through all the muck she determined to keep focused on the Father. Constantly, her life reminded me that "underneath are the everlasting arms."[1] We'd finish the night praying and casting our burdens on the One who cares for us.

She was such a soft place to land each night.

My fellow teachers were more than just colleagues.

Carol could read me when I didn't speak. The compassion in her eyes often encouraged me to take the next step. Nicole was a rare friend who could experience pain with you. Most friends try to fix it or make it go away. I've been guilty. It's a natural tendency to shy away from our loved one's pain because it hurts to see them so devastated. But Nicole and Claire weren't wigged out at my sorrow. They would stand in the empty hall to pray powerful prayers over me as my grief spilled out in deep sobs.

There were others. Parents and coworkers alike surrounded me with a quiet love by sending me notes or doing their best to help with my challenging class. My Crestview family represented a living expression of the Body of Christ tending to one of their wounded.

My fellow teachers were more than just colleagues.

Even with a bouquet of beautiful people coloring my life, I struggled. Most of the time when invitations came, I wanted to curl up in my yellow room, pull the comforter over my head, and soak my pillows with tears for all the people and things that had been removed from me. But that would be a mistake, and I knew it. I forced myself to remember all the beautiful people God had *added* to my life because of this twist of circumstances. If God provided something for me to do, then I needed to walk through the door and trust Him to help me through the evening.

In the end, God supplied *all* my needs in *each* situation. Every time I ventured out, I grew, and it was good.

One day, God gave me a mental picture of the community where He'd placed me.

I saw myself lying on the cold ground, injured and bleeding from a terrible accident. One of my friends immediately placed my head gently in her lap and began to stroke my hair. One quickly ran to get me some water, while a third took off her jacket to put over me. Another person flagged down someone to call an ambulance, while another turned her pretty scarf into a tourniquet to bind my oozing gash. Someone held my hand, while one more called out to the Father on my behalf. Still another kept the crowd from staring at the ghastly sight.

No one tried to do it all, but each person simply obeyed the impression given to him or her by the Holy Spirit. Together, God used their individual efforts to orchestrate a completed ministry.

They didn't act like the evening news that often exploits another's tragedy to bring excitement and something new to gossip about in the hallway. They served as agents of God, nursing one of their fallen back to health.

What a mercy to be in their midst.

◦◦◦

WHAT I GAINED: Though many people had been removed from my life, God gifted me with an amazing community. I just needed to be willing to receive their help.

12

COURAGEOUS GRIEF

JP and I had been officially separated for four months. One stormy April night, the truth of my life hit me hard in the gut.

Before this night, JP's excuses and rejections existed in my mind as isolated events. For some unknown reason that rainy night, all those moments entered the courtroom of my mind to present their arguments as a full story. Gathered together, they created an incriminating closing statement. Reality demanded my attention and forced me to assimilate the truth. "Look at me. Listen when I tell you. He's not coming back—not tomorrow, not next month, not next school year . . . not ever."

⸝⸏⸝

How do you cry something into existence? You can't. That's the worst part. No matter how much your hollowed heart aches, there's nothing you can do to reverse it.

I related to Gary Sittser's book, *A Grace Disguised,* as he explained the void he felt after losing his mother, wife and daughter in a single car crash: "One enters the abyss of emptiness . . . If anything, this kind of emptiness fills one with dread and despair."[1]

Surviving the vast darkness seemed impossible.

I did the only thing I could think to do. I crawled into bed and grabbed the red Book. Yes, I always have a Bible close by. It's my lifeline—has been since I was a little girl. Mine has always been red and I don't know what I'd do without it. But this spring night, I didn't believe even the Bible could offer a single word that could stop my hyperventilating.

I searched page by page—nothing.

I tried again. Flipping. Eyes darting. Scouring the pages. Looking for even the slightest flicker of hope. Still nothing.

Just as I expected. God is great, but even He had nothing for me on a night like this. Long-term, yes, but help for right now? No.

I couldn't concentrate. All I could do was weep, hard and deep.

Yet I couldn't give up the search. Not because I was such a mighty warrior or a determined Christian. Desperation forced me. I couldn't bear the abyss.

I don't know how long I looked. And not one second did I really believe I'd find any comfort.

Until—my eyes landed hard on top of the inside column of the right-hand page in the book of Psalms.

I read, "Be merciful to me O God, be merciful to me. For my soul trusts in You; And in the shadow of Your wings will I make my refuge until these calamities have passed by. I will cry out to God Most High, To God who performs all things for me" (Psalm 57:1-2. NKJV).

My spinning world slammed to a halt. According to these verses, somehow, God would take the devastation of these events and make them perform *for* me, not *to* me. They wouldn't destroy me, but rather God would use them for me, for my gain.

In the meantime, I could hide. Hide under the shadow of His sheltering wings until the calamities were over. Yes, I supposed one day it would pass. Relief would come. *When?* I didn't know. But tonight, I would nestle in under His wings and find refuge.

My heart quieted its thumping, and my breathing synchronized with deep, untroubled breaths—in and out. In and out. The hypnotic swishing of the ceiling fan cooled my face as the salty teardrops evaporated from my cheeks. My eyelids felt heavy, and courage to turn off the light engulfed me in the room's darkness.

Abruptly, like a jolt of electricity, panic jarred and threatened again, and "the unknown" paraded around the room tormenting me. *"What will happen if . . .? Why did . . .? How will . . .? If only . . ."*

It's amazing how regular words (not so regular when penned by the Holy Spirit) can stop a parade of dread in its tracks. According to 2 Corinthians 10, I had the authority, through His word, to take thoughts captive.[2] Every time those paralyzing thoughts jumped up to march around my mind, God's word barricaded their procession. Like a commanding general, those verses ordered them to sit down and shut up. They obeyed because they had to.

As I focused on the scriptures, my insides steadied once again. I didn't need to have all the answers. I only needed to concentrate on what I knew to be true. I could call out to God for mercy. I could find refuge under his wings, and He would perform these things *for* me, not *to* me.

His watchful eye would more than suffice as my protector for the night.

❦

After acknowledging reality that night, the picture of my future began taking shape. Although still hazy and unclear in spots, I had enough information to recognize that my life's new landscape would not be what I'd hoped. I'd been snatched from my enjoyable, ordinary life, and thrown into a strange and stifling parallel universe.

I didn't like the new scene. It was as unpleasant as waking up on a scorching, hot beach, your clothes melted to your skin and humidity so thick you can barely breath. The blinding sun blocked my vision. *Where am I? How did I get here?* I felt like a wretched castaway scrambling from an incoming wave that threatened to soak me and wash away my meager bag of supplies.

That was how life looked to me.

Daily activities scurried on around me oblivious to the upheaval in my world. I felt disconnected and the effort required to engage felt too hard. I didn't want to connect. I wanted to go home to the refreshing breeze I had left behind.

No matter how I willed the return of the lush green and the cool shade of my past, it had disappeared with the same finality of a sandcastle that's been swept away by the tide. Life now required a harsh restart.

I still longed for our marriage to work and would do anything necessary to make it happen. But one day in Maryellen's office, she pointed out a penetrating detail that became more obvious each day. JP had stopped working on our marriage.

Yet, still I hoped.

During my next counseling session, I thought I'd struck gold. As Scott and I discussed different aspects of my marriage, he mentioned that perhaps JP and I were experiencing the seesaw effect. He explained it in parenting terms.

If one partner is lax in disciplining the children, the other parent feels it necessary to make up for it. He or she becomes exceptionally strict. But in response to the stronger discipline, the lenient parent becomes *more* lax, which in return causes the disciplinarian to clamp down on the rules all the more. Before long, they are upside down and totally out of whack.

That made perfect sense to me as I understood it, but I misinterpreted my counselor's point. He didn't mean if one person just stopped what they were doing then suddenly everything would be hunky-dory. He was simply explaining the principle.

At that moment, all I heard was a potential solution to my problem. I figured maybe somehow I had instigated JP's wild side by being overly . . . something. I wasn't sure what yet, but I would find out. I intended to own up to it and make it right. JP mentioned to my brother that he never felt good enough for me. Maybe this really was all my fault.

I couldn't wait to share my new discovery with JP. I decided to swing by the house on my way back to the Kellys' and share this breakthrough discovery with him immediately. My battered Camry floated down the highway with a spring in her motor all the way to the house. We might finally be going home soon. I confessed to God I was sorry for trying to be whatever it was that made JP turn away. I didn't want to be like that, and I'd do anything necessary to change.

As I pulled up to the house, I noticed an unfamiliar, red car parked in the driveway. It appeared rather lived in, and the car seat in the back told me the owner must have a child. At some point—certainly before I turned the doorknob—I should have put the clues together, but I didn't. Since this was still my house I bounded in, unannounced.

There was my husband standing nose-to-nose with the woman I'd seen in the photo. You know those trance-like moments when you feel like this must be someone else's life? Yeah, this qualified as that. He was handing her a small gift bag from a ladies' store. Obviously, I startled them. She took the gift and scampered out the door before I could even wrap my head around the scene.

And then there we were. Just the two of us.

Suddenly, the news I'd been bursting to share became woefully irrelevant. But I was so stupid I thought, "I didn't actually see them kissing so maybe it was nothing." Still, I was denying what was right in front of my face, preferring to find JP trustworthy.

He backed up my theory by blowing off her presence as nothing. "She just stopped by to say hi."

"Really. What was in the bag?"

"Oh, I just felt bad for her. She said she was having a really hard day." His voice had that aw-shucks sound. "She doesn't have much money, so I bought her a bottle of her favorite lotion." He said it all so nonchalantly and heroically like he expected me to jump up and down and clap for his thoughtfulness.

The anger I'd kept at bay all these months threatened to burst like a two-liter of Coke opened after a good shaking. My skin tingled. If I didn't speak my mind, an explosion would be easier to clean up.

"What about me? I AM YOUR WIFE." *There. I said it.* I had wanted to say it for months but didn't because it felt childish. After all, what kind of love relationship is it if you have to fight for your place?

"You do realize that I have no money. People from my school are chipping in just so I can survive. You don't have a clue where I'm sleeping at night. I haven't had glucose test-strips for my diabetes because I can't afford them, and you're buying some woman lotion because she 'had a tough day'?" The words flew off my tongue like shots from an expert marksman in target practice. My blood boiled. *The audacity.*

Some irrational place inside me still wanted to lobby for a place in his lineup of priorities. But the truth finally shouted louder. I repeated words of counsel my friend Liz Anne had given me. "I'm supposed to be your number one. Not third or fourth on your list. In fact, I don't even want to *be* on a list. A wife ought to be number one with *no one else* in line. If she's not, there is a problem." Captain Obvious here.

At this point, I wasn't even sure if I landed in the top twenty on his list, let alone number one. Truth had made its big entrance, and with it entered a crippling pain.

I proceeded to tell him the purpose for my visit. He listened with a whipped-puppy look. He was a jerk and he knew it.

"I'm sorry. I'll buy you some test-strips." He acted contrite, but even his shame was all about him. He complained of a guilty conscious as he shared more betrayal. This woman had gotten pregnant during their escapades, and JP had given her money for an abortion. Now he had that on his conscience too. He shared it like he expected me to feel sorry for him.

A piercing like none other penetrated my heart. No wonder he had no concern for my life.

I wanted to reject his offer to buy the strips, to tell him I didn't want or need anything from him. But pride had long left me. Test-strips were expensive. I was desperate. So I accepted. A part of me wanted to believe this was his care for me, but that thought quickly dissipated. This was just a way to appease his conscious and get rid of his current problem . . . me.

I followed him in my car to the store. In the past several months of being separated, the few times we went somewhere together were moments I cherished. Even with the strain, I loved being near him. But walking through the store this time was different. I finally turned the corner. I had to. I couldn't deny the facts anymore. JP showed no sign of repentance and no interest in working on our marriage. While I would hope with all hope that he would choose me again, I would no longer put my life on hold. Somehow, I'd move ahead. Without him.

I said, "Thanks for the strips."

I got in my car. He got in his. We drove away to our separate lives.

I'd put up a brave front during that discourse with JP. Once back in my car, though, I phoned my counselor. I rarely called him outside of my scheduled appointments, but I needed help. This last blow clawed at the already thin fabric of my soul, and I was holding it together by a thread.

Only a few moments earlier, I'd thought I possessed the missing piece to our restoration. But this last scene plummeted me down into a new canyon of pain I didn't know how to handle. *They had conceived a child together?*

All the pain of infertility and inadequacy squeezed my

heart so tight I could barely breathe.

Scott listened compassionately yet addressed the situation realistically. No more false hopes. No more "maybe next week." I needed to take time to grieve the loss. Truly grieve. It was time.

I confessed, "I don't think I have the strength. I'm not trying to be dramatic, but my heart feels like I won't survive."

Scott's voice was calm. "I assure you, Rebecca. You can do this. You need to. God will go with you every step. He's already there waiting for you."

As I hung up the phone, my mind reflected back to a few days earlier. The sovereign God was mercifully preparing me for this moment. Previously that week, I'd heard a sermon about grief. The preacher had said grief is like peeling back layers on your life. It's a terrifying process because we never know what we'll find.

In a voice moved by emotion, the preacher explained that God would never send you down into that pit of grief by yourself. It wouldn't matter how deep you were required to go. He'd already be there, waiting. Regardless of how ugly or nasty the situation, you didn't need to be afraid. He would be right beside you, holding you as you expose every single layer.

❦

I understand why people won't grieve. It takes tremendous courage and faith. I trembled at the thought, scared to begin. But I believed what Katie Davis Majors said in her book,

Daring to Hope, "A faith that trusts Him regardless of the outcome is real."[3]

I wanted that kind of faith. I didn't know what the outcome of grieving would be, but I wanted to trust Him. Even if . . .

Even if what? I didn't know, but I suppose that's what faith is. Trusting when I didn't know, when I couldn't see and when my heart felt too weak to continue.

So, I plunged into grief's deep end and allowed myself to mourn the loss of my marriage.

I did. Thank God, I did.

I started facing not just the facts but also the emotions and questions that accompanied it. I finally put the pieces together about the smell in my bungalow and the gadgets I saw on the mantel the day I popped in after Christmas. My husband was on drugs. He had a girlfriend. And they'd conceived a child together, something I was not able to do. That blindsided me and plunged me down an additional swirling vortex of pain I didn't know existed.

There I was . . . barren, ugly and exposed before God. Unwanted. Abandoned. Nothing to offer. I pictured myself standing in the middle of a busy street naked and dirty. As people rushed past me I pleaded with someone to help me, but no one gave me a second look as if I didn't exist. In my mind's eye, I caught sight of JP. Above the traffic and bustle he had heard me and looked up. Our eyes locked. And for a moment, time froze, and I thought I glimpsed compassion in his eyes. My heart quickened. But in a finger snap, his head turned and he walked away as if he'd never seen me before in his life.

My grief was ugly—twisted face, puffy eyes and swollen lips, deep guttural sounds that left my throat hoarse and dry, my body and mind exhausted.

Grief has stages. I had been living in the first phase for months. Denial.

Next in the lineup was the anger. Sittser explains, "Suffering does not allow us the luxury of keeping the question at a safe distance. Rather, suffering forces us to think about God's essential nature. Is God sovereign? Is God good? Can we trust him?"[4]

My questions came rolling in rapid-fire, releasing a hurricane of rage that scared me. My mind told me I shouldn't be mad at God or JP, but I was so angry I didn't care. *Why did God let me marry him? I prayed more earnestly for JP than for anyone else in my whole life. How exactly does prayer work anyway? Years I've prayed, yet he's as cold and empty today as ever.*

❧

Grief takes time and patience. Three more stages awaited me: bargaining, resignation or depression and, finally, acceptance. I had dipped my toe into each of these stages, but only from the shoreline. It was time to dive in deep.

I didn't know much, but I knew not to run from the grieving. Some people avoid it or say they "refuse to go there", but there is no denying it anymore. Pretending the grief didn't exist would only cause me to remain in one of the stages. I knew people who lived in a perpetual state of denial or anger or depression. Because they cut themselves off from reality, those around them suffered. I didn't want that to be me. I did my best to embrace it and trusted God to be there waiting for me.

The last thing the Enemy wanted was for me to be healthy. He knows the prize that awaits whole people on the other side of grief, and it shakes him to the core. Joseph said it best in Genesis 50:20, "ye thought evil against me, but God meant it unto Good."

Unfortunately, grief doesn't come and go in a neat little package. The five stages typically come in a distinct order, but just because I'd made it through one of them didn't mean it wouldn't come back around another day. I needed to know that so when it happened I would understand it was normal. The scary forest of grief felt dark and I couldn't imagine ever escaping. But I held on to this fact: Christ was my Savior. I had a Guide.

For several days, I have no recollection of what took place. Eventually, I visited my parents in Florida to share with them the newly revealed details of JP's relationship. Up until this point, my dad had displayed patience and grace in hopes that JP and I would reconcile. He enjoyed JP and loved him like a son. I often grieved my dad's loss of a relationship he loved.

When I told them about my latest discoveries, I could almost see the visible change in my dad. He was not derogatory or revengeful about it, but emotionally and mentally, it was as if he stood up, brushed himself off and moved on down the road.

I'd been reading in I Samuel 15 about the time King Saul was instructed to kill all the Amalekites and demolish everything that belonged to them. He killed most of the people, but he spared the king. He destroyed most everything, but he saved the best animals and goods.

Amazingly, when Samuel arrived, Saul acted as if he'd followed God's instructions. Even after Samuel confronted him with proof of the wrong, Saul continued making crazy excuses.

God told Samuel to inform Saul that He had rejected him as king. Samuel never saw Saul again and lamented deeply for him.

Finally, in I Samuel 16, God asks Samuel something like, "How long are you going to grieve over Saul? Get up and go anoint David as king!"

This story tapped me on the shoulder. JP had responded in ways similar to Saul. This last encounter revealed his intentions: he had no desire to change his lifestyle. I felt God saying to me, "How long will you grieve for JP? How many clues do I need to send you? It's time to let go, Rebecca."

My dad recognized it. His example confirmed what I felt God whispering to my heart. Limbo season had ended. Time to move on.

❦

Moving on was not something I took lightly. The last thing I wanted was for our marriage to be over. But the truth remained; it had been over for quite some time.

I didn't know that in the beginning. Those months of waiting had purpose. I needed to try every resource and possibility. I wanted to give my best effort and pray that God would change his heart. God hates divorce, and so do I, but unfortunately, marriage requires two willing parties. Time had come to release the hope of reconciliation.

❦

WHAT I GAINED: Grieving takes courage and faith, but God will not send me into that pit alone. He's already there waiting, and He will walk with me every step of the way.

13

CLEAN WOUNDS

"Do you believe time heals all wounds?"

I sat across from my counselor trying to decide if he had just asked me a trick question. I'd heard that statement a gazillion times over the years. The right answer must be yes.

According to this philosophy, if the days simply peeled off the calendar, eventually one day out of the blue, I'd wake up and say, "Well, whattaya know. I'm all better now."

Only one problem: *I didn't believe it.*

I debated answering yes just because I thought that's what I ought to say. But I'd been upfront with my counselor from the beginning. Why start hiding now? My head started shaking no before I blurted out, "No. I don't."

My counselor smiled. "You're right." Time doesn't heal all wounds."

I knew it. Glad I didn't fall for it.

He continued, "But it does heal all *clean* wounds."

I let that sit there for a minute . . . Something resonated with me about that statement.

❧

The school year ended. The divorce papers came during teacher post-planning week. Found them on my desk after I had slipped out of my classroom for a minute. I thought I'd prepared myself. But just as there is no way to understand what it's like to be married until you're actually married, there was no way to understand what it's like to see your heartfelt vow neutralized by a piece of paper with a seal on it. Until it happens.

My school offered me a new contract for the next school year with more responsibility to help me financially, and the Kellys graciously invited me to stay with them again. Grateful, I accepted both. These offers would allow me to be in Atlanta next fall while waiting to be assigned a date for our divorce hearing.

❧

A whole new barrage of inward hauntings developed over my summer months in Florida. It started the day I ran up to the post office to complete paperwork for my passport. The minute I read the question about relational status, my insides felt zapped the way your tongue does when you touch it to a live battery

I hated the thought of checking the "Divorced" box and being lumped into a huge nameless pile of statistics. My marriage vow was real to me. Divorce meant you gave up or you didn't take your commitment seriously. The box mocked me. *"Join the crowd. Tons of people get divorced. So what? Come on, Rebecca. Just forget it and move on like everyone else."*

I wanted to scream, "No. That's not true of me. My vow was sacred. I didn't want to give up. I tried so hard!"

The box stared up at me, unaffected. *"Too bad. It wasn't enough, was it? Yeah, sorry. Just check the blasted divorce box."*

While I argued with a small square on a piece of paper, a new problem rushed in when a young woman entered the room. She struggled to keep her baby occupied as she waited in line with the rest of us.

Her features mirrored the lady who stood in my living room nose-to-nose with my husband. Without warning, a rage and disgust simmered inside me. She reminded me of silent heroines in the movies. Usually, the men in the story have a clueless woman like me in the public eye, yet secretly steal away in the shadows to a mistress, to love on her and encourage her for caring for their child.

Regardless of how hard the clueless woman tries, the wandering man will always have a special bond with the mistress and child, a bond that could never be removed, and in my case, a bond I would never know. The volcano of pain and jealousy began to stir, ready to splash slime on every innocent person in the post office line.

The emotion made no sense to me. I had never met this woman before in my life. Where did these horrid feelings of envy and disgust come from, and what was I supposed to do with it?

I loved people and respected them as being created in the image of God. No matter who they were or what they looked like, I wanted to love them. I'd never experienced this level of hate and envy. The emotion—and the depth of that emotion—scared me.

This lady in the post office was just the first of many victims of my silent scorn. I detested the angst in my heart, but I didn't know how to stop.

I'd repent. Then I'd scold myself, determined to not think this way anymore. But every time I saw a woman who favored my husband's fling—especially if she had a child—the hate flared up like a ghastly rash. Back down in the filth I'd fall, and the cycle would start all over again.

My previous fear that I didn't really love God resurrected as Satan enjoyed another field day. Who could really love God and feel such loathing for His workmanship? Once again, I was trapped in a vicious cycle I couldn't escape, and I needed outside help. I turned to my counselor for guidance.

Scott didn't act alarmed by my recent thoughts. In fact, it seemed he couldn't wait till I was finished to share a magnificent truth.

"Rebecca, I want you to imagine yourself running through the woods being chased by a bear."

I closed my eyes and placed myself in the thick. It was only imaginary, but I could hear the snapping of twigs and crunching leaves. I felt the ragged branches and briars grabbing at my skin. I sensed the bear gaining on me, my legs filled with lead.

He continued the scenario. "You spot a cabin across a field. Running with all your might, you hear the beast closing the gap. The cabin is almost within reach but so is he—so close you can feel his breath. You make it to the cabin and bar the door shut just as the grizzly swipes his paw at your back."

My heart pounded at the thought.

"Even though you're safe inside, your heart is still racing and you're gasping to catch your breath. In a little while, if you look out the window and see the grizzly staring back at you or hear him trying to enter the cabin, those feelings of hysteria and fear will overtake you again. You would quickly re-live the whole chasing scene. In fact, if you heard a branch scrape against the window, it may remind you of the bear's claw and send you into another panic, even though your mind knows a branch will not harm you."

I agreed.

Scott explained it would take time for my heart not to respond first to the emotional upheaval. But as time passed, those feelings would subside. Eventually, I'd be able to hear a branch scrape on the window without terror racing through my bones.

He said it was much the same way with the women who favored the mistress.

A Stone Mountain-sized boulder rolled off my chest as he assured me that my desire to love people was real. The lady at the post office had represented an awful experience in my life. It was actually quite natural to feel distaste in someone who symbolized shattering loss.

Understanding the root of these feelings equipped me to deal with them. In fact, once I comprehended that they stemmed from an experience and not a person, I felt sorry for JP's mistress. No doubt, her heart ached to be loved unconditionally as did mine. I wondered how different her life would've been if she'd known Jesus.

෴

Despite the occasional breakthrough, the rest of the summer, more doubts and questions assaulted my psyche. How could I trust myself to make wise decisions when I flubbed the one I'd prayed about more than anything in my whole life?

I wondered who I was supposed to be without JP. I hadn't expected such a loss of identity. Gerry Sittser explains it like this, "Catastrophic loss is like undergoing an amputation of our identity. It is not like the literal amputation of a limb. Rather . . . [i]t is the amputation of the self we once were or wanted to be, the self we can no longer be or become."[1]

I didn't even know my name. When JP asked me to be his wife, I unreservedly released my maiden name to show my commitment to become one with him. I'd been Mrs. Rebecca Smith for years. He wanted someone else now. I felt ashamed and desperate to continue using his name, yet changing mine would create so many awkward moments for people trying to remember what to call me. It felt like a lose-lose situation.

I realized in a few short months I'd face another issue. We would stand before a judge who'd sign our divorce request, and I would no longer be legally married to JP. For the last decade, I had put myself under his leadership. I never regretted that because I believe whole-heartedly that is God's intention for marriage.

But now my loyal heart didn't have a clue how to be *un*-loyal. My head may know I didn't have a husband, but how would I revamp my thinking, both mentally and emotionally, to believe it?

Then there was the unprotected part. I mustered up the courage to remove my wedding rings. I loved those rings. But besides the sting of removal, their absence left me open game to the opposite sex. I was alone in the huge city away from family. My left hand shouted, "Hey! Here I am. I've got no one to fall back on, no one to protect me. So, y'all come and scare the yoo-hoo out of me."

With all my heart, I wanted to handle this divorce with God's love and grace. But as we moved closer to the end of the road, I discovered more irritating predicaments I'd be forced to address. JP had ditched the scene to higher, more comfortable ground and left me to deal with the mess. That angered me like a hornet being chased from its hive.

Once again, I repented of my bitterness, hoping to move forward. But the negative thoughts plagued me continually. That's when I learned I hadn't really done the true work of forgiveness.

On the front end of the forgiveness subject, I needed to understand something. Forgiveness was not the same as reconciliation. Jesus said to forgive those who trespass against us. He never commanded us to reconcile.

While reconciliation remains His ultimate desire, He understands an important truth. Reconciling requires more than one person. God would never hold me accountable for an action that depended on another person's willingness to obey. That would be cruel and unreasonable. Anyone can forgive, but the only one who can reconcile a relationship is the person who broke it.

So how does one do the work of forgiveness?

Ephesians 4:32 commands us to forgive as Christ forgave us. Naturally, the question would be, "So then how did Christ forgive?"

My counselor took me to Colossians 2:14-15, "By canceling the record of debt that stood against us with its legal demands. This he set aside, nailing it to the cross. He disarmed the rulers and authorities, and put them to open shame, by triumphing over them in him" (ESV).

The first principle was important. Forgiveness didn't mean acting like a wrong didn't happen. The Colossians passage describes an ordinance, *listing* our sins. No sweeping it under the rug and playing like all the world was puppy dogs and roses.

That was not what Christ did, and He didn't ask me to do that either. Rather, forgiveness was quite the opposite. It was acknowledging the wrongs done against me, to the point of writing it down.

Scott urged me to make a list with three columns. The first column was the "Who" list. He instructed me to catalogue every person I needed to forgive. That seemed easy enough. Honestly, the list had been subconsciously imprinted in my mind for months.

The second column needed to be titled "What." Next to each person's name, I described the act that needed to be forgiven. I struggled with that column as I relived the hurtful moments.

Seeing the offenses in black and white felt akin to someone removing a bandage from a badly infected wound. It smelled, looked disgusting and made me feel squeamish. But the fact that I had the courage to peel back the soiled dressing filled me with relief, a comfort in having faced the pain head on.

I wondered at the purpose of the third column. The first two lists seemed to cover the bases.

The last column was to be titled "How." In that space I needed to explain how each one of the offenses made me *feel...* My grip tightened and the pencil hovered over the paper like repelling magnets.

I kept telling myself, "It's only words. Just write them." I had whispered most of these adjectives secretly to myself in the past, so why the deep resistance? I couldn't explain the mammoth difference between stating it, either mentally or out loud, and actually writing it down. While they sound like similar actions, they were indeed distinct. Writing the words on paper required admitting the power of another over me. It exposed my vulnerability. First, I'd been wooed.

Then, I'd been rejected and humiliated. I had been fooled and *used.*

Making it past this third column in the forgiveness process was a benchmark. But one more step remained. The verse also described the handwriting against you being blotted out and nailed to the cross—the cross where Christ traded His spotless life for my ugly sin. To be pursued with such a public, audacious act of sacrifice made my heart blush.

If Christ could forgive me, then could I not forgive?

Hot tears bubbled up from deep within my soul, and I tasted the salty liquid as it ran to the corners of my lips. This last column produced the deep purging my counselor referred to in his "clean wound" statement. It's the holler after touching your finger on the hot pan. It's the release after throwing up your guts. It's the deep satisfying breaths after a hard workout.

But a question arose. What if JP or someone else repeated these painful acts? What then? Could I forgive again?

The Bible said I needed to be willing to forgive seventy times seven.[2] It didn't seem fair to include such an unconditional statement. Only one thing gently pushed me forward toward this final stage of forgiveness: the fact that Christ publicly endured excruciating mental, emotional, physical, spiritual and social anguish for *my* gain.

Embracing the cross was the only way forgiveness made sense. It was on that beautiful-ugly cross where I nailed those writings of offense, knowing Christ had borne the repercussions of all that I'd suffered. Each time I endured the shame, He experienced it with me. Now He asked me to forgive the perpetrator and allow Him to bear the burden. I released my list as I pictured it nailed to His cross. The sins blotted out.

But something still wasn't right. I had another person to forgive . . .

⁓

To suggest that God needed to be forgiven sounded blasphemous. I remember sitting in the midst of majestic mountain scenery, the white puffy clouds drifting through the sky. In awe, I observed God's beautiful creation.

One minute, I praised Him for His handiwork, but the massive mountains and expansive sky taunted me. If God could speak such majesty into existence, why wouldn't He bring my husband back? Or why didn't He protect me from JP in the first place?

The identical feelings I had toward JP about being wooed and then abandoned rose up. It felt like God baited me into trusting Him and then slipped out a trap door leaving me to fend for myself. I wanted to shake my fist at him. *If you're so big and mighty then why did you let Evil win? Are you part monster? I trusted You, and You failed me.*

God did not fail me. My head knew that. He'd been so good to me. But I couldn't justify the pain He allowed.

I needed to go through this forgiveness process with God as the "Who."

And so, I placed God's name in the "Who" column and I

unleashed my angst upon Him. I learned He could handle anything I heaved His way. He knows I don't understand. He knows my frame. That I'm dust.[3] He's not insensitive to my suffering. Repeatedly in His word He invites His children to pour out our hearts to Him.[4]

Forgiveness didn't happen in a few minutes of a written exercise. Much like grief, I visited it often, but in time the bitterness dissipated, and peace came instead.

෬ᚑᚑᎽ

To forgive was no light task. It required humility to admit how much *I* need forgiveness, and it required trust that God's plan was best. Perhaps forgiving another is the greatest test of faith. For me, it meant releasing my guarded (and sometimes even cherished) pain. I no longer had the privilege of nursing my wounds as the victim. Yet in time, I was no longer stuck in the deteriorating pit of bitterness. I dumped all the gunk at the cross—at the feet of my Jesus— in exchange for healing and wholeness.

Indeed, time does heal all *clean* wounds.

෬ᚑᚑᎽ

WHAT I GAINED: The true work of forgiveness is a definite process. It was hard, but worth the struggle, because time does heal all *clean* wounds.

14

ALONE, BUT NOT BY MYSELF

Sweat dribbled down all three of our faces as we pushed and shoved my prized Ethan Allen couch up the Kellys' massive staircase to my suite. Donny, the Kellys' gardener/handyman, got roped into helping Stephanie, the Kellys' college-aged daughter, and me muscle the thing from the barn into the house and up the impossible staircase.

Once JP's intention to divorce was revealed, Mr. and Mrs. Kelly suggested I make the suite more my own. I couldn't have been more thrilled. Their home felt like a luxurious hotel, but at some point, no matter how beautiful a place is, you just want to go home. My strong nesting instincts couldn't wait to put my personal touches on the space. Maybe I would finally be able to relax and allow my mind a place to belong.

Several months earlier my friends, Tonya, Terrie and Jim, along with my brother Rodney—who drove up from

Florida and back the same day because I needed him—had helped move my half of the belongings out of the bungalow I used to call home. Mr. Kelly offered to store them in one of their outbuildings until my life straightened out.

Now, our muscles screamed for relief as Donny, Stephanie and I tried to figure out a way to round two tight corners into my room. No matter how many ways we tried, that prodigal couch refused to enter the space. I'm not one to give up, but I would've abandoned the mission several attempts earlier out of courtesy to Donny.

When Donny showed up at the Kellys' for work, he did whatever crazy tasks anyone asked him. This time however, I think he came close to jumping over the banister to end the madness. But Stephanie would have none of it. Her clenched determination urged us to keep trying. Suddenly, with our strength and spirit waning, the walls seemingly stepped aside as the couch fell through the doorway.

We cheered. We high-fived. We collapsed. And Stephanie and I thanked God. Stephanie was a kindred soul and intuitively knew that having my things nestled about me would infuse a new hopefulness and sense of normalcy into my life. Each item looked as though it'd been special ordered to complement the room. My heart snuggled into the space like it was made for me before the foundations of the world.

⌇

With the summer ended, the start of a new school year

ushered in a fresh crop of children and a brand-new grade for me. (Crestview graciously offered me the higher grade-level because it paid more.) While the curriculum would be new, the students would not. I'd taught these beauties a few years earlier, and a warm familiarity filled the classroom.

Things were looking up . . . on the outside.

The shock had worn off for those around me. People had grown accustomed to my new way of life, and from outward appearances, the last decade of my life vanished as if it had never existed. From what others saw, I looked fine. I laughed and played games. I entered into conversations. But inside I ached.

How would life ever be okay again? I'd been so sure that God's plan for my life included JP. I didn't know how to move on or even where to begin. My mind obsessed with thoughts of him, somehow *only* recalling the things I loved and desperately missed. Rarely did I remember the troubled times.

Soon, a new attitude crept into my soul. Not a weepy, or even angry feeling. I would've known what to do with that. No, my hurt turned fatalistic and sneering. Why should I love or care? It would only lead to more suffocating hurt. I was afraid to dream because that only splashed black ink over my delicate masterpiece.

But almost in the same breath, I'd burst with thankfulness over God's creative provision and tenderness. The miracles He'd done for me—I wouldn't have even believed they were true if I hadn't experienced them myself.

The ache and the cynicism battled constantly against the

gratitude and the process left me drained.

⚭

After a particularly pleasant day at school, I jumped in my car to head home, and my cell phone rang. It was my mom. She faithfully called to check on me and listen to my daily happenings. I answered the phone and began to prattle. My voice lilted and laughed as I relayed the crazy events of the day. I should have noticed her stillness on the other end.

When I ended my spiel, she said, "I just wanted to let you know it came today."

I had no idea what she meant.

She explained the official order from the judge had come in their mail. JP had sent it to my parents' house since he still didn't know where I lived. The summons notified me of the hearing date and place to finalize the divorce.

Logically, I shouldn't have been upset. I'd already begun living my life as if the divorce had already happened. But my heart didn't give a flip what my mind thought was logical. The date gave the vague reality substance. Divorce would soon be more than a "one day," and in matter of weeks, I was going to be a divorcée.

I could almost see myself spiraling down the black hole. But this time, I was prepared. Over the last several months, during moments of deep struggle, I'd learned to call for help and admit, "Hey, I'm really struggling here, can we talk for a minute?"

I rushed in the door to share my news with Mrs. Kelly,

my confidant and prayer warrior, only to remember they'd be out of town for the night. No worries. I called Claire. Her phone rang and rang. No answer. I tried Tonya; not home. Christy; unavailable. On down the list I went. I couldn't reach a soul.

I was alone in a huge, silent house . . .

As bedtime approached, I invited Belle, the Kellys' golden retriever, upstairs to be with me. Belle loved when someone forgot to close the kitchen door. Then she could sneak out of her designated space to roam other parts of the house.

This would be a win-win. Belle would get a little treat, and I'd have something to cuddle for the long night ahead. She quickly followed me up the steps and into my room.

Perfect.

About the time I settled into bed, Belle got up and wandered to the door. *That was odd.* I sang out her name. She didn't come. I traipsed down the hall and sweet-talked her to follow me. She curled up next to me for about the amount of time it took me to crawl back in bed—and then started the routine all over again.

After several attempts to get her to stay, I finally resigned myself to the fact that I couldn't even get the dog to hang with me.

Just the time you think you might understand what God is trying to teach you, He changes up the test. God had a new lesson for me to learn this time. I looked up. *Okay, God. I'm sensing You want me to learn that when there is no one, You will be with me.*

Instead of masking the solitude I tried to embrace it. But as I turned out the lights, fear covered me like a collapsed tent. This divorce thing was really happening and the permanence of it mocked my faith. I had believed and prayed that God would mend the shreds of our lives into a beautiful new fabric, but He hadn't.

That hope was gone.

I pulled out my CD player. For the last several months, I'd listened to the old hymn "Be Still My Soul" every day while getting dressed for work.

Be still my soul the Lord is on your side

I repeated that over and over. He is *for* me, not against me.

Bear patiently the cross of grief or pain.

The author had obviously understood. I wasn't the first to experience these feelings and wouldn't be the last.

Leave to thy God to order and provide

I was so tired of trying to figure it all out.

In every change He faithful will remain.

Someone who will remain. I relished the thought.

But my favorite line went like this:

Be still my soul, the waves and wind still know the Voice who ruled them while He dwelt below.[1]

The same God who made the wind and waves obey Him was the same God who controlled my days.

Fear couldn't suffocate as long as these truths rang in my ears. I pulled my CD player near the bed, as far as its chord would reach. Then I lay as close to the edge of my bed as I could without falling off. I hung my arm over the side to push play as I turned out the lights.

With the song filling the silence, I hugged my pillow while tears slid down my face. I wondered how I'd ever get to sleep if I had to keep reaching down to hit the play button.

As the last note began to sound, I uncurled my pillow and started to reach for the play button, when suddenly the song began to repeat automatically. I held my breath the next time to see if it would happen again. Time and again the song replayed without me pushing the button. *Did God come down here Himself to push the button for me?* I had no idea how the song continued to repeat, but I snuggled up to the thought that when no one else could come, He had come Himself to sit with me.

Later, I discovered that my CD player had a repeat button. Somehow, in the dark, I "accidentally" hit that button. However, after years of owning this player no one will convince me that my finding this feature on accident, on that particular night, was a coincidence.

He orchestrated my solitude so that He could prove to me a vital point. While He often used others to come to my aid, He was plenty capable Himself.

WHAT I GAINED: When all human help is absent, God will come.

15

TAB FOR THE WIN!

My parents drove up the night before the divorce. I had mixed emotions about them coming all the way up from Florida for the event. But several people close to me suggested I take some time off and head down to Florida after the official signing. I thought it a bit overkill but figured I should listen. After a few days, I'd get a one-way ticket back to Atlanta and begin my new life as a single woman.

Once I got my parents settled, I lay in bed wondering what to think. I felt nothing. Not dread. Not sadness. Not relief. I remembered being more nervous about getting married than I was about signing divorce papers.

My biggest concern regarding the next day was what to wear. How does one dress for a divorce? I had never been to one. Should I wear a dress? Fancy or plain? Maybe pants would be more appropriate? My mom picked out my fuchsia silk dress. It seemed a bit much, but I was tired of trying to figure it out, so I gladly agreed.

The next day, I grabbed a few things for the trip south and an outfit to change into for the ride home. After the hearing, we planned to stop by the hospital to say good-bye to the Kellys. Their granddaughter had been in a terrible accident and hung between life and death.

ᴄ⎯ᴏᴏ⎯ᴐ

The appointment was early in the morning, so we grabbed a biscuit and headed downtown. I started feeling a little nervous, but I chatted easily with my parents as we found our way through the parking garage. The closer we came to the courtroom, the more my insides began to tremble.

My mom felt the shift in the atmosphere too. Understanding the gravity of the situation and her tender emotions—she decided to wait in the lobby. She'd let my dad handle this one with me. I convinced myself I'd be fine. I simply needed to focus on doing the next thing. Find the elevator. Find the right floor. Locate the judge's chamber. Go through the metal detector. Find a seat on the long bench in the hall outside the chamber door. Laugh at my dad trying to get through the detector. Think, *He's such a sweet, kind man, so good-natured and easy. I didn't think I needed my parents here, but I'm so glad I didn't have to come alone. I can't believe this is happening. I can't believe JP doesn't want us anymore.*

My thoughts were abruptly interrupted at the sight of JP getting off the elevator. I tried to focus back on my dad who still couldn't make it past the security guard. He had removed every article of clothing possible without it getting embarrassing. The line behind him grew. He jokingly told the man, "If you can find it, you can *have* it." Everyone in the room let out a chuckle and seemed thankful for the humorous distraction.

JP looked handsome. My mom had picked out the right dress, and I was thankful she had come. I needed her intuition. JP obviously put thought into what he wore. As he entered the room he said, "Hello Beck."

The familiarity and tenderness in his voice made it hard to breathe, like someone had forced my head underwater. As he walked toward, me I just expected him to join me on the bench. Instead, he continued past me and found a seat on the opposite side of the hall.

Suddenly, all of my previous "oh, this is no big deal" mentality dissolved into oblivion. The reality that we were no longer one flesh stabbed me, creating a wound as fresh and deep as the first day. My heart drummed in my chest. My throat ached. I fought the urge to be near him at any cost.

People often speculate what they would do if their spouse cheated on them. Most of the time, they make bold statements of how they would cut their mate out of their life without a blink. I no doubt joined the tough-guy talk before I'd been forced to deal with the reality. Today, I wanted anything but the chosen solution.

God's beautiful creation of marriage makes husband and wife one flesh. JP was embroidered on my soul. Even after several months of knowing this day would come, I still was not prepared be *un*-one with him. I didn't know *how*. Being so close to him and yet so far felt like my heart was being plucked apart stitch by stitch. But from this day forward, that is exactly how it would be. I sat still, wishing to blend into the scenery. Despite my effort to buck up, tears slipped down my cheeks, staining my silk dress.

When our group number was called, we stood to enter the judge's chamber. My heart mourned to see how many others were there for the same reason. One lady hadn't seen or heard from her husband in several years. According to the guidelines of official abandonment, she was able to divorce him without his knowledge. Another man appeared with the official papers from his wife agreeing to end their union. She hadn't even bothered to come.

There were others. The whole scene resembled a line for to getting a driver's license renewed, not for disavowing a once beloved mate. It felt disgustedly sacrilegious to the holiness of marriage, yet there I was right in the middle of the pack.

In appearance, I looked just like them, but inside I screamed and writhed. *No. This is not what I want.* The judge barely even looked up when decreeing each divorce official with his stamp.

I found my dad and sat next to him. God knew how desperately I needed him today. He was a stable force, equipped to endure my pain. I tried to match his courageous demeanor despite the tears cascading down my stonewalled face.

I wondered why I was the only one in the room crying. I imagined people thought I was being childish and ridiculous for overreacting. Yet to me, this was the saddest day of my life. A covenant I'd made before God was being legally broken.

When the judge called our names, my stomach fluttered nervously. My mind rehearsed the questions I'd heard the judge ask the couples who'd gone before us. He will ask, "if you agree . . ." *No. I don't agree. But wait. If you say you don't agree does that mean you're willing to live with an unfaithful husband. No. That is not God's plan for my life or for JP's life. So, under those circumstances . . .*

Out of my mouth I heard the words, "I agree." At that moment, the judge looked up from his mound of paperwork, and we locked eyes. For a split second, I caught what I thought was a tinge of humanity and tenderness. But he quickly dropped his head to add his signature to the document and moved us through like a piece of machinery in an assembly line. Maybe he had to do it that way to continue his awful task of granting divorces. Before I could swallow, a new couple had been called.

Just like that, it was done. It was barely 10 a.m.

Eventually, there was nothing left to do but walk away. As we exited the courthouse, the sun shined and birds chirped, but inside an inky darkness shrouded my heart. I couldn't bear the thought of parting.

I turned to hug JP. He genuinely returned the embrace and added a deep kiss on my cheek. I spun toward my mother before I melted into slush. As I walked down the path, her hands flew to her mouth and she quickly turned the other direction.

What had caused her drastic reaction? I looked over my shoulder to see my dad and now ex-husband in a bear hug, both of them sobbing. I guess my dad couldn't simply walk away either. He had been brave long enough.

The finality. The permanence.

I felt my heart being ripped out of my chest.

The mystery of iniquity baffled me.

⚬

My parents and I headed to the hospital to check on the Kellys' granddaughter before leaving town. I was hemorrhaging inside, but so were the Kellys. I wanted to pull myself together to focus on their needs for the next several minutes. The sting was turning numb and the tears to glaze. I managed to stay strong in the crowd, but every time I was alone the tears seeped out.

Mrs. Kelly, even in her own pain and exhaustion, sensed it. Regardless of the words that were said or the makeup over my eyes, she knew. The tenderness in her eyes revealed it all.

As we prepared to leave, I mentioned I was so thirsty. Immediately, both my mom and dad dug out the change I needed for the vending machine. It warmed my heart and reminded me how blessed I was to have them with me. I headed down the hall toward the vending area when Mrs. Kelly yelled down the hall, "And Rebecca, they have TAB."

No way.

꘎

Teachers, parents and friends all intuitively know the unwritten rule. When a student falls down on the playground, the teacher sends them to the water fountain to let the cold-water aid in helping them regain composure. When a nightmare wakes a young darling, a cool drink quells the tears. When a burdened friend shows up at your door, a cup of coffee or hot tea releases the tension and encourages the soul.

For years TAB has been my treat. When I was fourteen years old, I became an insulin dependent diabetic. One of the few items a diabetic can consume without restraint is diet soda. I often claimed Psalm 103:5 "He satisfieth thy mouth with good things so thy youth is renewed like the eagles." When others grabbed dessert, I reached for a TAB. When my heart ached, a nice cold TAB soothed like aloe on a blistering sunburn.

As a young girl living in my parents' home, if I was out of TAB, I asked God for it. I made it a game with God not to ask my parents for it outright. I wanted Him to supply it.

We would be driving home, and I'd pray, "God will you please remind my mom or dad to ask me if I have any TAB?"

Did He really care enough about me to answer such a silly prayer? He did, and I found Him irresistible. Invariably, they'd ask, and we'd stop to pick some up.

As years passed, TAB became more difficult to find. It took a backseat to the new Diet Coke. Eventually, vending machines and jiffy marts stopped carrying the liquid gold and replaced it with the newer drink. So, when Mrs. Kelly told me this vending machine had TAB, I knew it was Him.

It's our secret.

An ice-cold TAB in an unfamiliar location shouts to me, "Rebecca, it's me, God. This is for you, my darling. I knew you'd be here. I knew your heart would be broken. It's not much, but I thought this might make you feel better. I love you."

It meant more to me than air to a drowning man.

⁓

WHAT I GAINED: No matter how bankrupt my soul had become, riches were found in the everlasting arms of Jesus.

16

THE NOTE

I thought I was prepared. I'd been living without JP for almost a year. During that time, nothing in my circumstances had changed. I lived in the same upstairs suite, worked at the same job, went to the same church. The only thing different now was a signed paper that classified me as divorced. But the finality of that little paper demoralized my strongest efforts to live business as usual. C.S. Lewis was right when he said, "There is nothing we can do with suffering except to suffer it."[1]

Waves of grief crashed about at unusual and unexpected times. My lack of composure stretched the few days at my parents' home into two weeks. While chatting with a friend or eating a meal with the family, out of nowhere, the tears would come rolling down my face like raindrops on a windowpane. No expression change. Just tears. I wanted to use my young niece Krista's excuse, "I'm not crying. My eyes are just leaking."

Every time a stranger asked me if I was married, my tongue thickened, and my brain dissipated into a fog. I couldn't bring myself to say no because I had been and still wanted to be. I couldn't say yes because I wasn't anymore. That left the dilemma of wondering if I should explain that I was divorced. I despised that label. I didn't want to be lumped in among those who tried marriage on like a disposable raincoat. When marriage stopped being fun or satisfying, they'd just thrown it away or traded in the old model for an upgrade.

Instead, I wanted to explain how strongly I believed in marriage and how I hated divorce and how even though I was divorced, it wasn't God's plan and . . . [deep breath]. All the poor soul wanted to know was if I was married. A simple yes or no would have sufficed.

The last several months, a new understanding awakened in me. All the times I'd been quick to make an assessment of someone's character or lot in life based on what I could see or the sliver of information I knew revealed my shallowness. People are much more than a checked box.

Now that I walked the path of a "stained reputation," the awareness that things are not as they appear became more than just a nice thing to say. Seeing people and loving them past what appeared on the outside or whatever label society had smacked on their backs as they hobbled through life's rough patches became a new way of relating for me.

~∞~

I don't remember much of those two weeks I spent with my parents in Florida after my court date, except that I received a letter in the mail from JP.

Strange.

He said he didn't deserve me. One day, he knew God would give me someone worthy of me. *Worthy of me?* He wanted me to know that if I ever needed anything, he was only a phone call away. *If I needed anything? Yes, I needed something. I needed him to keep his vow before God and me.*

It made no sense. What kind of guy cheats on his wife repeatedly and then says, "Hey babe, I'm here if you need anything?"

In a bizarre way, that letter jolted me from the trance of the emotional parting a few days earlier and deposited a good dose of reality back into my memory bank. Not long after it came, I found the courage to buy my plane ticket back to Georgia.

<hr/>

The morning of my departure, the questions and the fears lurked around the room before I even opened my eyes. A sick butterflies-in-the-stomach feeling swept over me.

Getting on that plane signified the start of a new, unwelcomed chapter in my life. The outward grief period needed to be replaced by accepting and dealing with my current reality. I dreaded facing life as a divorced, single woman. I dreaded facing students, coworkers and friends.

Bottom line—I dreaded facing life. But it was time.

As I prepared to leave that morning, every move took determined effort to continue, like trying to rollerblade through a mile-long wind tunnel. The temptation to chuck the whole thing and crawl back into my childhood bed met me around every corner.

As time to leave drew near, I gathered up my bags to load them in the car. When I opened the back door, I stumbled onto a disturbing scene. It took me a moment to take it all in.

At the back doorstep, a fuzzy gray kitten lay whimpering in obvious distress. The feline was positioned as if someone had purposely laid it there in hopes we could help. I scanned the neighborhood to see where the kitten had come from or who had delivered it, all the while listening to its pitiful, frail meowing.

Nothing appeared wrong with the little bundle on the outside. But it was too weak to lift its small head. Every little peep begged for help. The kitten was dying before my eyes. The nurturer in me wanted to pick it up and promise that everything would be okay. But that was a promise I couldn't guarantee. And if I didn't keep moving, I'd risk missing my plane. The lump in my throat I'd been trying to swallow all morning grew larger with each meow.

My mom saw the little fella and verbalized my thoughts as her motherly instincts flew into action. She grabbed a blanket and some milk, and then she tenderly lifted its head in an effort to get it to it drink.

I couldn't bear to watch this helpless animal die. I hated anything to suffer, but especially today. The death of my marriage and the rejection of the one I loved were all the death I could bear at the moment. The sadness of my recent experiences was a bottled-up river ready to burst through a dam too weak to hold. I caressed the kitten, trying to understand where this animal had come from. Was this someone's idea of a cruel joke? I felt the Enemy laughing, tempting me to succumb to the idea that life is too fragile to care.

I wished I could slip into my parents' backyard and dissolve into the earth.

As my heart contemplated the idea, my mom hollered, "Rebecca. Come look at this." Her voice sounded urgent. I had been in and out of the kitchen all morning long and had failed to notice a piece of scratch paper she pointed to on the kitchen countertop—a note scribbled in my dad's handwriting.

My dad doesn't write notes . . .

The last note I remember getting from him came when I was a young girl. On the days he made my school lunch, he'd write the same little message on my paper lunch bag in the form of a math problem. 2 good + 2 be = 4 gotten.

My dad's work schedule required him to leave before the sun peeked over the horizon that morning. He didn't want to wake me to say goodbye, so he left me this note instead.

It read, *"Jesus never fails, and our God is still on His throne."* The emotion I'd been holding back all morning now rolled down my cheeks because I knew the credibility of the author.

He'd survived his share of heartache. For two years, he nursed his dying wife through a painful rare disease, while trying to care for his three young children. He gritted through widowhood until he married my mom. Soon my brother Rodney and I were born. Yet after all these years, after all the disappointments and sadness, God was in charge of it all and Jesus had never failed him, not even one minute. It was my dad's way of letting me know that God was in control of my life and He would not fail *me* either.

I looked heavenward. The Enemy had torn at my fragile state all morning, squeezing the air out of my hope until it lay as limp and frail as the dying kitten. My dad's message had parachuted out of nowhere, like a warrior coming to snatch me from the arms of defeat.

The note provided the knot I needed at the end of the rope to keep from slipping off. God sees. He knows. He cares. He wins. God cares about this little kitten, too. I could keep moving forward. I carefully folded the note and tucked it in my wallet.

My mom and I put the little gray bundle in the laundry room on a soft carpet with a bowl of milk at its head. We both gave it a gentle stroke and jumped into the car.

We rode in silence, afraid our quivering voices would expose the feelings we sought to keep at bay. Most of our energy was used to keep the lumps *in* our throats and our outward appearance courageous. Every time panic threatened, I would rehearse the words from my dad's note. Eventually, my shaky, fragile state morphed into a dream-like existence. The kind of numb you get when you're performing the function of living, but it feels like it's not really you.

My mom called a few days after I settled back in Georgia. She explained that when she made it back from the airport, the kitten had died in her arms.

We both cried.

But I clung to the truth of the note. *Jesus never fails, and our God is still on His throne.*

⌒○⌒

WHAT I GAINED: I could never say it enough: *Jesus never fails, and our God is still on His throne.*

17

A SEAT RESERVED FOR YOU

My new life took off like a shot. Days full and exhausting, mixed with nights loaded down with lesson preparations for the next day of teaching fourth grade, a grade I hadn't taught before. My school didn't follow a set curriculum, and that required the teachers to do massive prep work.

I still had so many questions for God and no time or energy to explore them. I wanted to cry out to Him, *God, I've prayed until I'm blue. Have you not heard a word I've been saying?*

Frustration ruled. *What in the world has happened to me? I'm divorced—I still can't believe it. I'm living with strangers. I'm teaching a grade I never wanted to teach. And all I've ever wanted to be was a wife and a mother and to serve you. Is that so awful?*

I hinted at blaming God for creating these desires inside me and then denying me of them.

But how could I blame Him? He'd gone overboard to

take such detailed care of me. Then I'd weep out of shame for asking, for not trusting, for not being content. I tried to acknowledge my frailty and figure out how to live abundantly with the massive void in my life.

Every day, I expected that this would be the day I'd understand, or the day JP would get right, or the day God would send me a husband who loved Him like I did and we could serve Him together. But that day didn't come.

I knew the verse about all things working together for good.[1] One day, yes, life would work out, or so I'd been told. But I still had to walk and be and live today. "What do I do now?" kept rolling around in my head.

I dreaded the future when I considered the fact that my life consisted solely of studying my brains out all night, so I could squeak by the hours teaching, just so I could make it home in time to study my brains out again, the routine interrupted only by lonely, dull weekends. Like a mouse on the wheel, the cycle never ended. The faster I ran, the more feverish the wheel turned. I missed being a wife, and my desire to be a mother got tied up and shoved up into the dark attic.

This wild-haired idea kept creeping up that maybe JP would repent of his lifestyle and come back. Each time the thought reappeared, momentum in my heart grew. Soon, I became bent on it happening.

I didn't know if I was wrong or foolish or right to keep praying and believing. I determined to pray for him more fervently than ever before.

But I felt trapped in the paradox of not giving up on a

miracle and moving on with my life. Simple joys reminded me of JP at every turn. I took those reminders as a signal to pray.

Doggonit. I was stuck.

No, I was obsessed.

Time to call for help.

After I explained my new fixation to my counselor, he asked me to think through the story of Mary and Martha. I knew the scene well. The sisters invited Jesus into their home. During His visit, Mary sat at Jesus' feet, while Martha bustled about trying to fix everything for others. She complained to Jesus and asked Him to make Mary help her.

But Jesus didn't. Instead, He said, "Martha, Martha, you are worried and troubled about many things. But one thing is needed, and Mary has chosen that good part."[2]

A light turned on like flipping on a flood light in a dark alley. My whole life I'd thought of myself as a Mary. I longed to sit at Jesus' feet and know Him more. But in this instance, I was acting like Martha "worried and anxious," thinking it all depended on me, and trying to "fix" JP with my prayers.

When my remedies didn't work, I was left with the residual frustration and exhaustion. I couldn't move anywhere as long as I focused on being JP's solution.

All the while, Jesus longed for me to sit at His feet and hear what He wanted to teach me about the situation. God could work on JP all by Himself. What He really wanted from me was *me*.

I wanted Him too. I'd loved Him since I was a little girl.

He was my best friend, but it was time to know Him more.

Over the last several months, I'd spent hours at the park, walking the trail and talking to Jesus. After my walk, I would grab my journal and head to *our* bench down by the pond. Sometimes as I walked around the bend, I could see someone sitting in our spot. *God, would You make them move so I can sit with You?*

Sure enough, as I moved toward the bench, the invaders would gather their things and relocate to a new spot. God cleared the bench just for us. The other park-goers didn't realize that bench had been reserved.

I sat with Him on our bench, filling journal after journal, peeling back the complex layers of my heart. I held nothing back. Every whim exposed. Every question and doubt I aimed at His goodness and plan came bursting out on the bench. Yet still He sat with me. And I loved Him for it.

Time on the bench felt like a friend's deep hug, letting my body relax and feel safe. Sometimes it reminded me of the way a child feels when a teacher tenderly moves the bangs out of her face after a tussle on the playground, followed by a loving pat on the head and a lifting of the hair from under her collar. At the bench, I was *seen* and *heard* even in my mess. And He loved me still.

I echoed what Sara Haggerty describes, "But when I scooted up next to Him, when His nearness felt as real to me as my own hands, I wanted it all . . . . When I was near enough to Him to smell His skin, the rest of the world and my circumstances faded into gray. He was *that good*."[3]

Yes. He was.

My seat next to Him was the most important place in the world. He had reserved it, set it apart and barred anyone else from occupying it so I could be near Him.

He had *benched* me, right next to Himself.

Once my obsession with JP turned toward the One who would never leave me nor forsake me, onto the One who gave His life to be in an intimate relationship with me, then He was finally able to reveal the part of Himself He'd been longing for me to know. The part that adored and treasured me more than any husband or friend could.

❦

As the new year flipped up on the calendar, newness sprouted in my heart too. A baby spring in my step appeared. For the first time in months, excitement and anticipation of the future fluttered its way into my emotional basket. Almost daily, new discoveries about my life and my old way of thinking surfaced.

It's embarrassing to admit, but all my life I'd been striving to be in His "elite" club by following certain man-made rules. As if, right? Like God gives out "Disciple of the Year" awards.

Discovering how God delighted in things that delighted me created a reaction. The chains, and the monkeys, and the baggage started falling off leaving me lighter than I even knew possible.

With my pride dissipating, for the first time in my life, I understood why people raised their hands in church during the song service. Before now, I guess I assumed it was because people wanted to make a spectacle of themselves. Perhaps sometimes that's true, but now I understood a new, pure motivation.

Beth Moore describes it in *Audacious*: "Nobody can tell you what to do with the things that cost you. They are yours. Like every scar, they are a part of how you are marked with originality. But you have the right, if you audaciously insist, to pour every last ounce on the feet of Jesus."[4]

It didn't matter to me if anyone understood what I was doing because Jesus did. He had been too present, too tender, too attentive to me. During a praise and worship service, I could no longer sit unmoved and stoic. My hands lifted in deep adoration for His supreme worthiness and in acknowledgment of my utter dependence and desire for Him.

~oༀ~

The Enemy of my soul fought hard to beat me down and write the story of my life. Sometimes, it seemed like he was winning. He tried diligently to prevent me from moving forward, and I know why.

For months, a change had been taking place just below the surface of my heart. Finally, the pendulum began to swing. The questions were running their course and leading me back to a deeper love relationship with Jesus. Satan would've preferred I exit the scene before the good part. He didn't want me to experience the growth and the joy God had waiting for me.

Now I know, when it feels the darkest, dawn must be on its way.

❧

WHAT I GAINED: It was not my job to "fix" JP through my prayers. I needed to fix my eyes on Jesus, sit in the seat He reserved especially for me and listen to Him.

18

KIDNAPPED

I found myself in a crowded football stadium sitting next to my friend's tall, good-looking brother. When he finagled his way to the seat next to me, I knew the game he was interested in wasn't on the field.

I wasn't stupid. At least I didn't *think* so.

He flashed me a charming smile and "accidentally" (not at all) bumped shoulders with me, tantalizing me to play along. Just a gentle bump sent a fuzzy feeling that started in my stomach and traveled throughout my whole body to my fingertips. I joined in the game before I could think otherwise.

Wedding rings would have warded off his playful bantering, but they'd been tucked away in the bottom of my jewelry dish weeks ago. Once again, I realized that to the outside world I was fair game. I no longer had my husband's protection, either physically or mentally. Without the shield of marital commitment surrounding me, I felt as unsafe as a dust particle being blown into wet paint.

We weren't on a date. His sister had simply invited me to join her at the game. But that tidbit of knowledge didn't stop my weak heart from soaring at the thought. I wasn't prepared for his doting. I even knew he meant nothing serious by the flirting, yet my heart fluttered every time he leaned in close to tell me something or laughed at my half-witted effort to be cutesy. The mere fact that he acted interested in me made my heart clap and coo like a baby tasting ice cream for the first time.

It scared me.

ﻬ

Being drawn to someone other than my sworn love felt foreign and disloyal. For years, I'd guarded my heart and focused it on one man. After the divorce, I needed to know God's thoughts on whether I was free to date or ever marry again.

I assumed I had a solid conviction regarding remarriage, since I had grown up in church and attended Bible college. But assumption alone wasn't adequate for me when it meant my real-life relationship with God. I needed to know without a doubt. I re-evaluated and searched every passage I could find on God's guidelines regarding marriage after divorce. I sought counsel and devoured sermons on the topic.

Eventually, my conclusion matched my original theory.

According to Matthew 19, because of my husband's repeated infidelity, I had God's nod of approval to marry again if the opportunity ever arose.

So spiritually speaking, my conscience was fine with the flirting, but the shock of experiencing it sent conflicting waves rumbling through my soul. It felt wrong and uncomfortable yet alluring and pleasing all at the same time.

I made a mental note of how quickly my heart was captured by another's playful banter, and I thought I had conquered vulnerability by merely acknowledging it existed. After all, isn't that half the battle? Once you know you're gullible, you're ready for it.

Should the time come for me to go on, say, a real date, I'd remember. I'd be ready.

‿◦‿

In God's mercy, He let me start by dipping my heart in the dating water months before the stadium encounter. My first "would you like to go out with me" offer came from a total stranger. Our seats landed beside each other on a flight. His respect and interest in my thoughts and ideas fed my soul like water being poured on a wilted pansy. I felt myself blossoming right there in seat 24b.

When our plane landed, I wanted nothing more than to accept his invitation to play golf the next day, but I was not yet officially divorced. The title "Mrs." still belonged to me. It took every bit of discipline to decline. I knew it sounded rigid and letter-of-the-law-ish to refrain from dating until the divorce was final, but it was important to me to honor my vow to God until the very end.

I have no regrets.

In fleeting moments between the pain, I imagined dating a thousand times. I didn't want anything serious. My heart still belonged to JP, but perhaps golf and a burger would be a nice way to spend a Saturday. I longed for JP to find out that another man found me appealing. In truth, I hoped knowing would eat him alive from the inside out.

I couldn't ignore the desire to date, so I tried to guard my heart. Best I could.

But nothing could have prepared me for my first date after the divorce.

❦

My phone rang. On the other line was Jake, a friend of the Kellys I'd met on an outing with them. "I was wondering if you'd like to go with me to…"

My mind swirled. I tried to steady my thoughts like holding a hot bowl of soup on a bumpy car ride.

According to Mr. & Mrs. Kelly, although Jake was in his 30s, it's likely he was new at this dating thing. Brand-new. Like maybe this was his first attempt. I was honored that he would ask me, but inside, my heart fell. We had nothing in common, and the attraction-level measured negative on the scale.

A surge of anger overtook me the minute the invite spilled out. I wanted to spit fire at JP. He should have been here to protect me from this. But he wasn't, and I had a nervous man on the line who had risked rejection waiting for my answer.

It felt like I'd been in a dressing room between outfit changes, when suddenly the door flung open. There I stood. Exposed. JP had guarded the door for years. Now he'd abandoned the post, leaving me unprotected and open for the hunt.

I didn't want to say yes, but I accepted the invitation. I needed to try this.

The day arrived like any other Saturday. But as the time drew near for me to get ready, a shroud of sadness and confusion clung to me. Frustrated tears started rolling down my face quicker than I could brush them away. *How did I get to this place in my life, deciding what to wear, getting fixed up for someone other than my husband?* It felt unnatural and weird.

My head knew I was single, but my heart still felt very much attached. I wanted to pound JP into corn meal for leaving me.

As I was about to walk downstairs to meet Jake, the words of my friend Christy came rushing back to me. She was younger and more acquainted with the current dating scene. She warned me, "Rebecca, don't ever go anywhere without twenty bucks in your wallet. You never know when you might need to call a cab or something."

I rarely had cash on hand, but thankfully I'd just gotten

paid. I grabbed a twenty, took a deep breath and dove into the dating scene like jumping on the count of three into a freezing lake. On the way down the steps, I tried to pump myself up. *This will be fine. How bad could it be? He's got a nice convertible. It will be over in no time.*

It felt awkward, like first dates do, but my heaviness whooshed away as we dashed through downtown Atlanta in Jake's shiny blue convertible. I could do this. I felt God's mercy lift my spirits as my hair blew aimlessly in the wind.

His nerves and my uncertainty crept in, but we limped along in conversation. Thankfully, a group of singles from his church joined us at dinner and helped pass the time with much needed distraction.

Finally, the waiter dropped off everyone's checks encased in black servers' books. A welcomed sight. The date would be winding down soon, and I'd be home within the hour.

Everyone immediately grabbed their checks and whipped out their credit cards.

Everyone, except Jake.

The waiter came and went several times in hopes, no doubt, that he'd find our bill ready to be processed.

Not so, my friend.

The check rested in the middle of the table for several minutes. The longer it sat, the more glaring it became. I'd said everything I could think of to say, asked every question on every topic I could pull out of my repertoire of friendly. With each answer I nodded, smiled, and thought, *"Doesn't he see the check?"*

Several more minutes clicked off the clock, and in between my nodding I screamed in my head, *"It's right there in front of him like a lit-up scoreboard. Why won't he pick it up?"* He'd paid for the first part of the date, and I knew money was not an issue for him. I tried to will it in my heart, *"Pick up the check. Please."* I begged. I pleaded. I sent up SOS signals to the Father above.

I'm not a mind reader, but from the gentle looks sent my way by the rest of the group they tried to will the same thing. The little black book loomed larger by the minute. I didn't want to embarrass him, but by this time Awkward hadn't just joined us; it had pulled up a recliner and chomped popcorn as everyone—except Jake—squirmed.

Eventually, I couldn't take it anymore. I whipped out my twenty and stuck it in the black book.

That seemed to snap him to attention. He followed suit and stuck some cash inside. After carefully perusing the bill he gave me back $1.67 for his part of the meal.

I forced my legs to walk and not run to the car; I could smell the end in sight. But after I paid for my own meal, he seemed to open up even more and decided to take the scenic route home. Several grueling hours after we'd left home, he returned me to the Kellys' driveway.

I should have invited him in to say hello to the family, but I couldn't bear the thought. Like a freed bird escaping from her blue convertible cage, I flew up to my room, flopped on the bed and let out a long, arduous groan.

With my face buried in my hands, I could have sworn I heard God belly laughing. Soon I joined right in. Despite the staggeringly long and difficult afternoon, I knew His presence was with me from start to finish. The sheer mercy of sending me out with money I rarely carry, coupled with the pure misery and awkwardness of spending eons with a person in which I have nothing in common, lessened the blow in a twisted funny sort of way. Together, these bizarre details gave me a gentle initiation into the world of dating as a once-married-now-single woman.

～∞～

After the first few months of being officially single, I began to hear it from a variety of sources. Close friends, acquaintances, even family.

"Rebecca, I know this great guy . . ."

My parents were the first to bring it up. My chin hit the floor as my dad raved about a newcomer he'd met in his Sunday school class. This guy Brett was part owner of a semi-professional sports team, the community loved him and he came faithfully to church. He sounded too good to be true.

My dad had *never* involved himself in my dating life, let alone handpicked someone for me. He became obsessed with me meeting him. I'd be lying if I said I didn't imagine myself with a well-to-do Prince Charming sweeping me off my feet, chauffeuring me around in a golf cart chariot as we roamed the field to watch his team play. But then again, the too-good-to-be-true thing . . .

～∞～

A few other vanilla-flavored dates were in the books before I was able to meet my parents' pick for me. The crazy coincidence (nothing is coincidence) turned out that Mr. Kelly had business dealings with Brett. That seemed odd. What would be the chance that both my dad and Mr. Kelly would know the same man? They barely knew each other themselves—and that connection was only through me.

With the meeting set, my nerves started unraveling. This felt different from the other dates I'd been on. Taking a bird's eye view, it appeared to me that God had piloted our paths to cross, while my dad and Mr. Kelly, the two most important men in my life, had served as fellow first mates on the excursion.

Mr. Kelly arranged for us to be introduced at an event he was attending. We spent several minutes throughout the evening chatting. I left the function feeling repelled and fascinated at the same time. Brett definitely intrigued me and managed to commandeer my thoughts for days afterward.

We discovered we'd both be in North Florida during my spring break and tentatively set up a time to go out. Every day, I waited with great anticipation for him to follow through with the details. Before I realized it, I had become fixated with worrying if he would call.

My dad joined the fray. He was as giddy as a schoolgirl who'd just plucked the last daisy petal landing on "he loves me." He hounded me day after day asking if Brett had called.

The stronger my feelings for Brett grew, the more distant

I felt from God. Suddenly, this stable ground I'd enjoyed walking on the last few months had changed. Uncertainty and a feeling that something was wrong crept back into my life. This path felt like a slippery frozen pond, and with each step, I anticipated the sound of crackling ice. But I couldn't decipher the source of the angst.

The week was almost up before the call finally came. He made arrangements for my family and me to attend his team's game. Then he'd find me after the game and take me to grab a bite to eat. I told him, "That sounds great. I'll see you then," and hung up.

I thought I'd feel better when he called. Instead, anxiety overpowered me. Not good anxiety, but anxious anxiety, the unhealthy kind that keeps you from eating and sleeping. My dad was a nervous wreck too, like maybe he held the winning lotto ticket and needed to deliver it to the store before he lost it. I'd never seen him act this way before.

The night finally came. My mom, dad and I headed to the arena. My brother would meet us there. With everyone's crazy schedules, I couldn't remember the last time we had enjoyed a night on the town together—and at a sporting event, our family's favorite pastime. We had no idea the beautiful memory God's mercy had afforded us.

We laughed at my dad barking out orders for us to get to the game on time. We cheered. And laughed more. They ate popcorn and hotdogs. I chewed my fingernails in nervous preparation for my pending date. As the clock ticked down, my heart began to thump so strong I could almost see it.

Brett's team squeaked out an exciting last-minute win,

and just like, that people began flooding out of the stadium. My brother joined the rush, while my parents and I stood wondering what to do next. My instructions from Brett had been, "Don't worry. I'll find you."

My dad's frenzy began building. He asked every person he saw with a walkie-talkie if they knew where he could find Brett. Dad led the charge to every nook and cranny of the stadium with mom and me dragging behind him. One time, he followed Brett through the crowd for ten minutes trying to catch him, only to discover he'd been trailing the wrong man.

As time wore on, my heart started sensing that tongue-on-the-battery feeling. There I stood in my new linen pantsuit as the crowded coliseum turned into a ghost town. My old buddies, Embarrassment and Shame, came to stand beside me until I couldn't take it one minute longer. I tried to give this guy the benefit of the doubt, but I could also take a hint.

I begged my dad to *please* go get the car. Only one guard remained in the huge lobby. If this Brett guy wanted to find me, I wasn't hard to spot. My mom joined in my plea, and my dad finally acquiesced to our request. I was humiliated and angry with myself for getting my hopes up. I wanted nothing more than to escape the scene.

When our car pulled into the circular drive, my legs couldn't move fast enough. I scooted in front of the headlights to take my usual seat behind the driver. Just as I grabbed the door handle, I heard the guard yell out, "Miss, wait. Are you looking for Mr. Boyd?"

I looked up to answer and saw a man through the glass wall entrance running down a huge flight of steps, tie and coat flapping. It was Brett with an entourage behind him. He called out my name. "Wait! Please wait!" He burst out he arena doors and stopped at more steps to catch his breath.

The scene entranced me. Watching this grown man running to find me before I rode off into the night felt like I was acting out a scene of a Hallmark movie.

As Brett made his way down the final flight of steps toward me, he apologized for his flawed plan. "Please forgive me. I'd still love to take you out, if it's not too late."

My dad slapped the car in park and jumped out with a grin wider than the Mississippi River.

Brett shook my dad's hand and asked, "May I kidnap your daughter for a while if I promise to bring her home safe and sound?" I felt my defensive heart turning into soft putty. His chivalrous display had not only charmed his way into my good graces, it had also swept me off my feet. Standing in the cool night air with a gentle breeze from heaven felt like the perfect night with the perfect man.

My dad answered with a lilt to his voice, "Kidnap her? You can have her!"

I never doubted my dad's love. This statement didn't offend. It stamped his approval of another man besides JP in my life. No one had worked harder than he had to see it happen.

Those were some of the last words I ever heard my dad say.

WHAT I GAINED: Don't allow your circumstances to distract you from embracing moments with those you hold dear.

19

UNLIKELY COMFORTERS

Brett whisked me away to a fun restaurant for the post-game celebration, and time slipped away like cotton candy evaporates in your mouth. It looked as if this last twist in the night's turns would lead to a memory worth dreaming about.

I excused myself to the ladies' room before we headed home. Alone for the first time, I smiled up at God. *Oh Lord, what an amazing night you've given me. Thank you. A million times, thank you.*

I glanced down at my cell phone and noticed several missed calls and one voicemail. Who would be calling me this late? I listened to the message. It was from Rodney's wife. "Hey, Becca. Sorry to bother you, but I wanted to let you know Rod said your mom and dad were in a wreck on the way home from the game. You should probably ask Brett to take you to the emergency room instead of home." Her voice sounded like a friend reminding you to stop by the dry cleaners on the way home.

My heart sank. Brett had just asked me if I wanted to travel with him a few towns over to watch his team the next night. Now I figured my parents would need me near if they were sore from the fender-bender. The disappointment I felt surprised me.

Brett gladly drove me to the hospital. I knew he was exhausted from the week's preparations. "You can just drop me off. It's late. I'm sure it's fine, and you know how slow emergency rooms are." I meant it. I didn't expect him to stay.

He abruptly rejected my offer. "No, It's dark out here. I'll walk you in."

I wasn't afraid, but oh, how nice it felt to be valued enough to be protected.

"And I want to make sure your parents are okay."

This guy. I liked him.

The person at the hospital desk directed us away from the ER waiting room to a separate room down the hall. "You have some other family members waiting for you."

That's strange. It's 1:00 in the morning. Why would other family be here, and why are they in a separate room?

As Brett and I followed her down the hall, I had concern on my face, but my heart still hadn't descended back to earth. My date with the man walking beside me still held my attention.

The nurse pushed open the door for us. Once I glimpsed my brother Rodney's pale, hopeless expression, I knew my sister-in-law's nonchalant message did not match the seriousness of the situation. My eyes scanned over to see my Uncle Buff and my cousin, Steven, who, in addition to being our cousin, was also my brother's best friend. He's the one Rod would call if he were ever desperate. They stared straight ahead with the same expressionless faces. Then it finally occurred to me. They wouldn't all be here if this were just a little car accident.

My eyes darted back to my brother. Someone mentioned that this was the best trauma hospital around. If anyone can help your dad, they can.

Trauma hospital? I wasn't thinking trauma. I assumed they'd been brought here because this was the hospital closest to the stadium. I blurted out. "Rodney, what happened?"

With eyes as big as blue china plates, he swallowed hard and started shaking his head before the words came out. "It's not good, Beck." Pause. He stared at the floor, his head still shaking. "It's not good." It was all he could muster.

No, God. Please, no.

While Brett and I ordered bruschetta and Diet Coke, a truck had run a red light that broadsided my dad's side of the car. He was in surgery for multiple fractures and internal bleeding. My mother, who suffered broken ribs and a collapsed lung was stable but in critical condition.

Those moments waiting for the doctor's report, I

convinced myself that God wouldn't take my dad. Not now. I urged everyone around me to have faith. Their fatalistic perspective exasperated me, like trying to put out a fire using a bucket with holes in it. I needed them to be strong. God wouldn't do this. Not so soon after losing JP. It had only been six months since we'd officially divorced. The healing had been slow but steady.

I pleaded with all my might to God for my dad's life to be spared. At times, I feared we might lose my mother as well. My emotional pendulum swung wild and fast between an intense belief that God would spare us this pain, and the possible horror that He might not.

Brett stayed by my side as wide-eyed as the rest of us. The doctor mistook him as my husband. Maybe it was the way I buried my head in his shoulder. Maybe it was the concern on his face. Or perhaps we just looked like a natural fit. Regardless, I couldn't imagine facing that experience alone. With him near me, I wasn't. He played the role of comforting mate well, and it felt sublime. The night's devastation forced our young relationship to fast-forward into seasoned couple. *Was it possible for one night to lead to a nightmarish ending and a fairytale beginning all at the same time?*

The surgeon pushed open the thick doors with an expression that matched the waiting room's ashen walls, and then he invited Rod and me into the hallway. Struggling to convey his findings, he spoke as if he'd just operated on his own father.

"Your dad was hurt very badly. I, uh . . . I've done all that I can do."

Done all you can do? What does that mean? "But he's still alive, right?"

"Technically, yes. But you kids have a decision to make. He won't live without a ventilator. And if he did, his life would be extremely painful."

As a young girl, I had envisioned a moment like this, and I dreaded being faced with such an awful choice. Yet here I was.

Suddenly, standing there next to my brother, I felt an inconceivable strength. God's grace and peace in the moment showed up bigger and stronger than confusion and hopelessness. We would not be spared the pain, but God would walk the path with us.

The doctor asked if we wanted to see him. Oh, my heart wanted to see him, yet I feared what he looked like. I checked Rodney's eyes. A special bond existed between us and we could tell what the other meant without saying a word. Yep, he was thinking the same thing. We gave each other the nod. We would be brave together.

Plus, I still wasn't convinced that everything had been done for my dad. The doctor said he was still alive. Maybe God would choose to perform a miracle.

With God's grace holding our hands, we walked down the hall to the operating room. When the doctor pushed open the doors, the scene seared itself into my memory. The nurses froze as Rodney and I walked in—like the big secret was out, and there was no other way to hide it. In that moment, the nightmare finally exposed itself. My fantasy world evaporated, and I realized God would not spare us the heartache. My dad lay on a gurney, tubes everywhere, and his right arm hung off the side of the table, limp.

My heart staggered as I imagined the terror of all he and my mom had experienced. I wondered. *Was he afraid? Did he wish all of his kids could be there with him? Was there anything he was aching to say to us?* Fear and sadness punched me in the stomach, and the strength that just walked me down the hall dissipated leaving me with jelly-filled legs.

But as quickly as changing a television channel, an overwhelming peace reframed the whole picture. Rod and I looked at each other. We both knew. Almost simultaneously we spoke—resolve and confidence welling up inside us. "He's not here."

True. A machine pumped air into my dad's lungs, but I had no doubt that he had left his earthly body. Sometime between 10:00 pm and the present, Ivan Clark Anderstrom had been catapulted from this life up to his new residence, Heaven—the place he'd longed for his whole life. The Spirit of God whispered to me, "Honey, you don't need to worry about your father. All his fear and pain have been replaced!" As we stood watching his earthly shell, he was probably telling his favorite joke to his mom, dad, and many others who had gone there before him.

My mind reflected on the last year and all the extra trips I'd made home. I thought those trips were a mere distraction from my troubles. Little did I know the treasure of time God had afforded me with my parents. I had no idea it would be some of the last memories we'd share, and I'm so grateful I learned to savor those moments and truly enjoy them. I shudder now to think how close I teetered on the edge of being emotionally absent during my dad's last days on earth. Grief almost stole the final bits of time God orchestrated for us to be together, but gratefulness rescued our days.

Rodney and I were certain dad was home, but we needed to consult with our older siblings, Ross, Rhonda and Reed, before giving permission to remove Dad from the ventilator. They all lived out of state, but we reached the guys within minutes. My sister, Rhonda, had recently started a career as a flight attendant and was out on a run. Her husband Jerry needed to track down her whereabouts, which would be a challenge in the middle of the night. Plus, Rhonda was a daddy's girl. The news needed to come from her husband.

We waited through the night as Jerry worked to locate my sister. He finally reached her in a small-town hotel with a tiny airport. Being the only flight attendant on duty, she was alone in a strange city. Jerry stayed on the phone with her as long as he could. Eventually, she was left alone in the silence with heartbreak as her only companion.

Rhonda would later tell us that she sobbed with uncontrollable abandon.

Her crushing grief reverberated around the tiny room so loudly she barely heard the knock on her door. At 3:30 a.m. Rhonda opened the door to a woman with long, dark hair, wearing a maid's uniform.

"Ma'am, I heard you crying." Her voice was tender and thick with accent. "Are you okay?"

Rhonda didn't care that maids don't work at three in the morning. She didn't care that she'd never seen her before that moment. All she cared about was that someone was there—a compassionate human who risked the unknown to comfort someone in deep distress.

That night a total stranger held my sister in her arms and let her weep.

Oh, the mercy and grace of God.

WHAT I GAINED: God's mercy and grace will be sufficient. Sometimes, He sends a first date or a maid in the middle of the night to be just the comfort we need.

20

VULNERABLE . . .

The next several days threw me into a tailspin of activity and emotions. With my mom clinging to life, I spent most of the time in the hospital with her, begging God afresh, "Please, don't take my mom, too." I couldn't bear the thought of losing both my parents. While family and friends flooded into town for the funeral, the quiet moments in the dark hospital room afforded my thoughts time to breathe.

I exhaled silent sobs as fear and confusion quickly filled the gaping hole left by my dad. He was the sweetest father a girl could ask for. His mild manner and jovial sense of humor made him loved by everyone. He had five children, and somehow, each of us thought we were his favorite. Even in the midst of tense, difficult circumstances, my dad's presence gave the impression that everything would be all right, and he possessed an uncanny ability to make us laugh even in the worst of times. I'd seen him cry only a few times—when he sang hymns, when he broke his ribs and when his dad died.

My father was the glue that held our family dynamic in place. Without him, life shattered into shards too fragmented to recognize. I grieved the loss of my family's identity and reason for gathering.

My breath caught when I thought of this new relationship with Brett like being the honored guest at a surprise party. From all outward appearances, my dad's last act on this earth involved ensuring we were together. Was this from God? If so, then why did I feel such uncertainty? Why did it feel the closer I got to Brett, the farther removed God seemed? The more I pondered it, the more my appetite subsided. My diabetes scrambled to keep up with the stress and erratic schedule. Once again, I turned sunken and skeleton-like.

I held my breath the day my siblings and I examined the remains of the mangled car. A chilling reality settled in my bones. I had come within seconds of occupying my usual spot behind my dad. My brother hugged me tight as we peered in to see that same seat crushed beyond recognition. Without a doubt, my life had been spared.

The whole night of the accident had been so uncharacteristic of my dad. I had no explanation. I felt compelled to trust that God was in control of it all. I needed to cling to each mercy He sent my way.

❦

The days ahead required more gumption than I'd ever needed in my entire life. While my dad was prepared to die spiritually, he was not prepared to die physically. At least we could find no evidence of it. We tore the house apart searching for insurance policies and safe deposit box information while experiencing a red-tape nightmare. All to little avail.

In the end, my mom would be left to support herself, a feat overwhelming amid the grief and recovery of her own broken body. But equal to my dad's strength was that of my mother. Her mottos throughout life were "Where there is a will, there is a way," and "When all else fails, laugh!" With her witty sense of humor and fierce resolve, I had watched her repeatedly press on during life's hardships.

But this experience had done more than knock the wind out of her. It had stolen her fight and crushed her will. Rodney and I tried to keep her home business afloat, but the time-sensitive requirements proved too much for us.

With yet another major loss, I feared my mother would give up on life—the grief and burden too great to bear. I made arrangements with my school to stay for several weeks to take care of her ailing body until she was well enough to be on her own. My sister, Rhonda, stayed to help as long as she could, but eventually she needed to fly home to her own family.

The pain of watching my mother suffer on top of the rest of the troubles forced me to dig into depths of soul I never even knew existed. We faced each day wondering how we'd make it till tomorrow. Wondering how to pay the bills.

Wondering how she could find a job in her condition. Gloom settled into every room. The whole house felt like it had been inundated with quicksand.

I survived by following a principle I'd learned earlier in the journey with JP: I lived one moment at a time and thanked God for everything I could think of. At least today we had a roof over our head and food on the table. I'd ask myself, *Can I just get out of bed to let the dog out?*

Yes.

Can I go brush my teeth?

Yes.

In my mom's presence, I pulled out every positive, upbeat word and smile I could muster. But deep in my heart, I had no idea how this could possibly turn out well. The mental battle of pushing aside the cares of tomorrow to focus on the blessing of the day exhausted me.

The more difficult life became, the more I relished time with Brett. I wondered if he'd hung the moon, and he seemed to think I'd had a part in hanging the stars. Time with Brett restored a glimmer of hope that perhaps life consisted of more than gigantic heartaches. The strange circumstances of our meeting led me to assume this was all part of God's plan to restore the years the wild locusts had eaten with JP.

All of that would have been wonderful except those head-over-heals feelings were mingled with doubts and red flags. As soon as they popped up, I'd smash those flags out of my mind with the hammer of remembering how my dad had literally died to see that Brett and I would be together.

I was falling for him—fast. And it scared me.

I wanted to run, but my feet seemed nailed to the floor. I begged God to help me understand what was happening. Was Brett a mere distraction to help ease the pain, or was I truly falling in love with the man God sent me? But if God sent him, why was my stomach in perpetual knots?

The stronger the attraction, the more red flags began appearing. I only verbalized the good parts to my mom and others around me, and I continued to excuse away the questions. Convinced that the circumstances around our dating could only come from God, I determined to do the right thing and love him through his flaws. Just like I did with JP.

Oh, I can't believe I just said that. Well, but this will be different.

‿◦‿

The more time we spent together, the stronger my physical attraction came. Brett had awakened desires in me that I'd pushed aside when JP left.

I begged God to stop teasing me with Brett. If we weren't supposed to be together, then why would he have brought him into my life in the first place? I didn't ask for it or manipulate it. It seemed like a cruel joke that He'd bring him into my life, allow me to fall crazy for him, and then snatch him away because being together wasn't really a good thing after all.

Then again, maybe doubts were simply wrinkles to work

through.

I didn't know.

One day over dinner, my news came spilling out to my friend Claire. "I think I'm going to marry him!" I regurgitated the whole story of our meeting, flowering on about my new love's qualities.

She nodded and smiled, and then putting her fork down, she stared right in my eyes. "What is your greatest apprehension about him?"

Whoa. I had expected a reaction more like, *Oh, Rebecca, I'm so happy for you,*

But that one question buoyed all my red flags from the depths, and I knew my answer before she even finished asking. I'd never voiced it out loud before. "Sometimes I think he lies to me."

Her smiles and nods excused themselves to wait in the car. She ignored any fear that I might be offended. "That is one area you *cannot* question, Rebecca."

I'm not sure what I expected her to do, but it didn't entail such a strong confrontation. I knew deep down she was right, no matter how crazy the circumstances of our meeting. But my heart was in so deep I didn't know if I cared. It terrified me that it didn't terrify me.

⟨∽⟩

Then came a weekend back in Atlanta. I'd taken a few days to spend with Brett at his home. Maybe it didn't look good to others, but I was a grown woman. I didn't believe in premarital sex, and he'd never made me feel uncomfortable or pressured me to do anything that violated my conscience. I stayed in the guest bedroom, so there was nothing to worry about except wholesome, uninterrupted time together.

One night, the rat race of life and emotional whirlwind of the last several days left us drained. Snuggled up next to each other on the couch we both dozed in and out of sleep. As I headed up to bed, Brett asked me what appeared to be a logical question. "Why don't we just sleep in the same room tonight? I sleep so much more soundly with you near me."

Immediately I said, "No." Although in my heart nothing sounded better.

He brought up a good point. "We're not going to do anything wrong. It's really no different than falling asleep on the couch together." He laughed. "It's just a lot more comfortable."

When you looked at it that way, it sounded reasonable enough. I had no intention of violating my principles, so what difference would it make? He continued the dialogue making stronger and more rational arguments to his point.

I did my best to articulate my hesitation, but he shot holes through every reason I presented. I couldn't put my finger on it, but regardless of how sensible and innocent it sounded, an uneasy feeling barricaded my agreement to the idea.

Brett huffed, obviously thinking me a silly, prudish girl. I wondered if he was right. I'd been so careful my whole life, setting up dating guidelines and boundaries as long as I could remember. *What good had it done me? My marriage had still been destroyed by sexual sin.*

As I reached the top of the stairs, I had a choice. Loosen up my rigid ideals and go left into comforting arms, or follow my heart's inward voice and turn right to my single bed. The lure pulled greater than I'd ever experienced. In light of Brett's arguments, my head couldn't explain why going to my own room felt right. Maybe I didn't need to be so unbending and cautious. Going left would be simple, just a few steps . . .

I turned right— in more ways than one—and my heart was at peace.

Maybe nothing immoral would have happened that night, but I have no doubt that crossing that simple line would've eventually erupted into a great chasm, sinking me deeper than I would've ever bargained for.

༄

Brett and I didn't last much longer. In a few weeks, we parted ways and my heart broke all over again. The further removed I became from the situation the more similarities I recognized between Brett and JP. He was just like JP—only with more money and a suit.

Fear of what was wrong with me rushed to the front of the line. *Why won't anyone love me for the duration? Why do I continue to choose destructive relationships?* I had seen the warnings, but I clung to the circumstances of our meeting as proof that God must have put us together. It felt like God pushed me into it. I didn't understand. Even after all that

God had done for me, once again, fear that I didn't really hear or know Him harassed me.

The combination of another shattered dream, the confusion of why I'd fallen heart-first into another unhealthy relationship and all the grief accompanying my parents' accident shoved me right back down the anguish trail. The path had grown so familiar I wondered if this would be my forever lot.

~~~

I needed to hear from God. The ocean's beautiful scene provided the perfect meeting place. Its massive creation always refocused my perspective on God's power.

With the beach nearly empty, I enjoyed the solitude as I roamed the shore and contemplated life. The uncertain future loomed overhead. I didn't trust myself to make good decisions about anything, and all the rejection and disappointment left my heart raw.

These thoughts rolled in and out as quickly as the waves crashing at my feet, when I heard a woman's voice behind me, "Excuse me. Miss?"

It startled me. I hadn't seen anyone come up. I scanned the area to see where she might have come from. We were standing quite a distance from the other beach-goers and a football field's length from the parking lot. Her outfit screamed *Lost*. She wore shorts and a t-shirt and carried a pair of heels in her hand.

She explained she was new in town and needed to find a

particular location. I tried to help her, and the next thing I knew, her life story came spilling out. Something about this woman warmed and encouraged me, and from her story, somehow we transitioned into mine. She listened intently, welcoming my words like a long-lost friend. I unleashed all my questions and fears without hesitation.

When I finished the run-down, she peered into my eyes, and in a big sister kind of way she said, "Be careful. And be patient. Your heart is very fragile and vulnerable right now."

Vulnerable? But I know God and His word. That insulated me from 'vulnerable,' right?

"You're not able to make good decisions."

My pride wanted to deny that statement, but I couldn't. She sure pegged me on that one.

"You're not ready for a relationship. You will be someday, but not yet. Trust me. I know, and I have the emotional scars to prove it. Your priority needs to be your healing."

The conversation died down. She thanked me and said she needed to get going. As she walked away, I stood there a minute watching the waves, trying to soak in her words of advice. Her boldness took me back. *Who was this woman?*

Suddenly, I remembered I had no idea where she had come from. I looked up to see which way she was heading, but she was nowhere in sight. I scanned every possible exit off the beach. She was gone.

To this day, I believe God sent me an angel. I have no proof. I suppose only in heaven will I know for sure. But her message resonated deep in my soul.

I thought I had exposed my vulnerability after my friend's brother flirted with me at the ball game.

Wrong.

I thought because I managed a few dates I was ready for the big league.

Wrong again.

Call it arrogant or crazy, but I hadn't seen myself as relationally vulnerable until that moment. But she was right. I needed to focus on healing and understanding why I kept choosing unhealthy relationships. I agonized over this question in perpetuum and begged God to show me what was wrong with me.

Eventually, like a Polaroid picture coming into focus, the answer emerged. In both cases of JP and Brett, I excused away alarming character flaws because of the *potential* I saw in them. I realized my problem.

I cannot. Marry someone. For his potential. The end.

It didn't matter if someone would be great someday or even if I loved him. Those were the wrong questions. I needed to ask, *"Do I want to be one with this man?"* Right this moment, in his current state, did our lives so match that I would welcome every part of him into every part of me?

I thank God for the two women he sent into my life—my friend Claire who forced me to verbalize my reservations and the stranger God sent to give me a mirror into my soul.

She was right. I wasn't ready. One day I would be. Just not today.

WHAT I GAINED: Before my vulnerable heart could enter a serious dating relationship, I needed to discover why I repeatedly chose unhealthy relationships. Instead of marrying someone for his potential I needed to ask myself, "Do I want to be *one* with him?

21

THE DOOR OF HOPE

There she stood, nestled in among the hedges at the end of the Kellys' driveway. Sculpted to resemble Rebekah at the well from Genesis 24, this beautiful statue of a woman in flowing concrete garments with a simple pot on her shoulders welcomed me home each night. Rain or shine, every time I saw this statue it reminded me of her story.

Abraham needed a wife for his son Isaac, so he instructed his servant to find her. The wise servant prayed to the God of Heaven for help and then devised a plan. When he arrived at his destination, he would ask a woman for a drink of water. The lady who went the extra mile by offering to water his camels would be the woman chosen. Sounds like a simple task until you realize how much water a camel drinks.

A young damsel named Rebekah approached the well. When she woke up that morning, she had no idea that by nightfall her life would be delightfully changed. Being at the well was nothing unusual for her. She showed up daily and fulfilled the task God had given her to do, regardless of how monotonous it may be.

When Abraham's servant asked her for a drink, her kind heart volunteered to give the camels a drink as well. *She wasn't so busy seeking a new life that she missed the one she was living at the moment.*

I desired to be like that— to embrace life's moments wholeheartedly and refresh the lives of others around me. But I wasn't, and I didn't know what to do about it.

I asked God to please renew my mind. Change my thinking. He had promised abundant life, but what exactly did that look like for me? I couldn't imagine that included being single. People would say to me, "Oh, Rebecca. God is going to bring you a wonderful man. I just know it!" But God never made that promise. What if I never married again? Then what? Somehow abundant life must still be possible.

That summer after my dad died, once my mom was stable enough to be on her own, Mr. & Mrs. Kelly offered to send me to London for two weeks to visit their daughter, Stephanie. Their generous invitation couldn't have come at a better time. The events and loss of recent weeks pushed me near the breaking point. Maybe they sensed it too. I knew this was a gift from God, like He was sending me on vacation with just Him. I didn't even consider saying no.

I wanted God to change me on this trip. There were questions I needed answered. *How do I do this "single" thing? What was I supposed to do with these intense desires to be a wife and a mother?* I didn't know how *not* to want that. But I was willing to learn if that was His will. I wanted Him most. I confirmed that just days before my flight out of the country.

Sitting in church one Sunday night, I felt estranged from God, like He was mad at me about something. I hated that feeling.

Just a couple of rows ahead of me sat a darling family. The wife snuggled under the arm of her handsome husband, and periodically glanced down at their three tow-headed children to ensure they were behaving.

I did what many people do when they observe a scene in which they wish to be inserted: I imagined their perfect life.

I deducted that they lived in one of those nice neighborhoods near the church, had family devotions every night and game night once a week. The wife was probably the woman of her husband's dreams, and somehow despite his busy schedule, he still found time to shower her with affection.

As I gathered all of that in my mind's eye, a profound thought dawned on me. If I possessed all I had just concocted but lived void of God—no matter what dream I imagined—none of it would be worth it. No man or child, alive or imaginary, could make me happy or replace my relationship with Him.

I wanted to be different when I returned from Europe. I wanted to know I was complete in Christ *alone*.

∽

The trip provided just the break I needed to keep from literally breaking. Stephanie and her roommate Lexi were the perfect hostesses. For the first time in months, I enjoyed frivolous pleasures, luxurious sites and long walks in beautiful parks. We watched movies and spied on the royals, ate new foods and slept 'til we wanted to get up.

I had forgotten how refreshing it was not to be so serious all the time. We had wonderful discussions, sometimes about trivial nonsense and sometimes of deep philosophical ideas. One day, Lexi shared a great observation she'd made. "If I'm not careful, I can go through a whole week and not live one moment of it."

That statement hit me hard. I think I'd gone through whole chunks of life without really living it. Most of my focus had been on doing everything right or planning for the future. I had missed the simple pleasures and ministry opportunities right before my eyes.

I slowly grasped this concept and began to live it out on the streets of London. Almost instantly, life became an adventure. Meeting people became more like a divine appointment then an interruption. I actually *saw* them. I smiled at everyone and jumped into conversations I would have previously avoided. Maybe they only needed a laugh we'd share, or maybe the encounter would be life changing.

My prayer became, *"Let my face reflect your love and joy, so everyone I meet will see how great You are, and that true hope only comes from You."*

By the trip's end, the tension knob on my life returned to a tolerable position. But as with most vacations, reality jerked me back to the daily grind and the unanswered questions.

I dreaded the coming year. The only thing that kept me moving forward was knowing that I was in the center of God's will for my life. Every time I wavered, I asked, *"Where else would you rather be? Really. Where?"*

All the other options faded fast when I realized anywhere else would be out of the place God had for me.

As much as my head grasped the idea, my heart was too tired to buck up and fall in line. I couldn't snap out of it. My attitude stunk—and I had all the guilt to prove it.

I longed to be content regardless of my life's circumstances, but I struggled with knowing what to do with the dreams and desires that had awakened in me. No matter how hard I tried to dismiss them, they hung around like the smell of cigarette smoke. A few months ago, I thought God had provided a happily-ever-after with Brett, but when that fell through and I lost my dad, I slipped deeper down into the pit. My hope had been denied one too many times, and I resigned myself to living in despair. That was no way to live and deep down I knew that.

I wanted to come to a place where, like Rebekah, I embraced each day as a gift from God, no matter how mundane or lonely. The weekends were the most difficult.

Every Friday night driving home from work, I'd ride past the local high school. I'd see the stadium lights and hear the band warming up for the football game. I could almost smell the fresh buttery popcorn and feel the fizz of the Diet Coke.

Oh, I miss my life. It hurts, Father.

I expected to hear Him say (not an audible voice, but an impression in my heart), "I know, honey. I'm sorry."

But that's not what I heard.

Repeatedly, the Spirit of God would impress Isaiah 43:18-19 on my heart: "Remember not the former things, neither consider the things of old. Behold, I will do a new thing; now it shall spring forth, shall ye not know it? I will even make a way in the wilderness, and rivers in the desert."

I'd respond, *"But God, I don't need new things. The old way wasn't easy, but it was okay. Maybe you thought you were doing me a favor, but I miss the old way something terrible."*

And I'd hear in my spirit, "Remember not the former things . . . Behold I will do a new thing."

In a lot of ways, I'd let go of JP, but I still hung onto my old life. I missed our friends. I missed the ball games and being part of a team. Regardless of my argument, God's message to me never wavered. He wasn't harsh or irritated, just steady and firm. God understood my sadness, but He loved me enough not to be manipulated by tears or pleas.

Back and forth we'd go. At first it felt like pouring

alcohol into tender wounds. But as I quoted His word, the sadness softened, and an anticipation of what God was doing stepped into its place. The more I embraced the verses, the shorter the arguments grew.

As much as I tried to embrace this "new thing" God was doing, I didn't know how to stop desiring something that God had placed in my heart to begin with. I knew it wasn't wrong to wish to be married or be a mother. God delights in those roles. He created them for goodness sake. But my obsession to have them and discontentment without them crossed the line into wrong.

If singleness was God's plan for me, then I'd strive to embrace it in hopes that one day my heart would want it as well.

That sounded noble and spiritual. Too bad I couldn't keep up my end of the deal. I tried my best to deny my desires, but when they surfaced in my unguarded thoughts, I sunk into despair for not being able to embrace this "new thing." After all He'd done for me, how could I be so ungrateful. I berated myself so God wouldn't have to, calling myself every low-down name I could muster.

My frustration turned into anger at God. I wanted to be obedient, but what did He expect from me? He's the one who made women with this innate desire to be a wife and a mother, so why did *I* feel guilty about desiring it? It was His fault and completely unfair.

Lashing out at God never made me feel better. It did, however, manage to pile on more shame and defeat. I felt trapped by the angst and panicky feeling that I'd never be free of this mental curse.

One day on my way to work, the answer appeared with the same surprise as an unexpected bouquet of flowers delivered to your door.

Without realizing it, I'd been living under the premise that since God gave me the desire then it was my right to be a wife and a mother. God was not disappointed in me for wanting what was holy and natural. My desire wasn't wrong but claiming it as an expected privilege was. I didn't need to deny them. I just needed to *surrender* them.

What a relief.

Now instead of trying to deny my desires, I could boldly acknowledge them and cast them at Jesus' feet. He encouraged me to express to Him how deeply it hurt. Although I didn't understand Him, I asked myself if I could trust Him to make the best plan for my life.

Yes. I could do that.

According to Psalm 139, every day was ordained for me before one of them came to be. I believed God had a specific plan for each day. On the long nights, I'd ask, "Okay God, what do you have planned for us tonight?"

I decided to embrace the moments as a gift.

Instead of viewing myself as child-less or husband-less, I began thinking in terms of child-free and husband-free. Being single allowed me to engage in things a family may hinder. Perhaps one day my life would be full of people again, and I'd long for quiet evenings.

Sometimes He'd come through with bizarre things. I found myself in unlikely places with people I barely knew. When I imagined looking down on my life, I chuckled. *What was I doing in this town or at this fundraiser?* It made no sense in the grand scheme. In the end, I just chalked it up to a new experience and a nice break from the routine. I had no idea how God was preparing me for my new thing.

While huge strides had been made in accepting singleness, I still longed for more. I felt cursed—like no matter how hard I ran the race I could only come in near the bottom of the pack. Obviously, I was missing something.

The time came when God began to open my eyes to see the picture behind the picture. And he used the arts to do it. It started with the movie *Annie*. I'd watched that film scores of times, but on this particular day, I saw a picture of myself.

Annie was a little orphan girl with nothing of material wealth to offer, but her uninhibited love became irresistible to a mega-wealthy man, Daddy Warbucks. Then, of course, an antagonistic trio showed up searching for her. They successfully used deceit to capture the orphan so they could use her for their own gain. Somehow Annie escaped long enough to buy herself a little time.

As I watched Annie scamper up the scaffolding to flee the selfish capturers, something inside me clicked. Daddy Warbucks adored that ragamuffin girl despite his efforts to avoid it. It delighted me to see the whimsy with which he used his power to enrich her life. Now, his girl was in life-threatening trouble. Left to herself, the enemy would overtake her.

But her enemies hadn't taken into account a man like Daddy Warbucks. He spared no expense to rescue her, digging into his own bank account and calling on every powerful resource available just to save this disheveled redhead.

I felt God say to me, "Rebecca, you mean *that* to Me. I adore you more than anything it may cost to prove it. I would spare no expense to rescue you from anything or anyone who tries to take you from Me. I can do anything I want, but I choose *you*."

To be the receiver of such an audacious love made me feel every bit as beautiful and worthy as I imagined Cinderella felt when I heard the story as a little girl. But this wasn't a fairytale. This was true.

But I never saw myself more clearly than when I read *The Scarlet Pimpernel* by Emma Orczy. The silly woman in the story was completely enamored with an unidentified hero. She boasted of his bravery to all who would listen, while she openly berated her fumbling husband (if you haven't read the book, a warning: spoilers ahead!). Yet all along, this dashing hero had been her husband in disguise, and she didn't even know it. His enduring love saved her scrawny hide despite her constant insults.

I felt God gently speak. "Rebecca, you're just like her. You are desperately searching for your hero, yet here I am right under your nose. I'm everything you could possibly imagine. Not only am I everything you'd ever want, but also, I'm crazy about you. I want you to know me. I won't ever leave you for someone better. You, Rebecca, are my darling."

Sometimes discoveries are made over time. Looking back through life, you may not remember exactly when you learned how to cook, but as an adult, you realize you're actually quite good at it. You have no idea what day you lost weight. At work, you don't remember transitioning from newbie to veteran or the day you stopped mourning over never wearing your cheerleading uniform again. Here's why—none of those things happened overnight.

But one day, you wake up and there you are—a great cook, a secure veteran employee, wearing a size six, happy you're watching the cheerleader's stunt instead of holding it on your shoulders. You take a quick look in the rear-view mirror of life and wonder how it all happened. The day started off as an ordinary day, but reflecting on where you were then and where you are now transports you to a moment of discovery.

My friend Claire told me one day, "Rebecca, it's like you are standing in the middle of a theater stage. It's pitch-black.

You can't even see your hand in front of you face. But you hear activity all around you—the shuffling of feet and the scooting of props into place. You feel a slight breeze or smell the shampooed hair of the stage crew as they rush past you, entering and exiting. Then one day God will flip on the lights, and there you'll be, standing in the middle of a perfectly dressed set and suddenly, you'll understand."

⌒○⌒

It was Valentine's Day. On my way to work, I mused over all these different thoughts. Suddenly like finding the perfect focus on a camera lens it all made sense. And these words fell into my heart.

The King of the Ages, my Prince, Adoniah,
Abba, Jehovah, Shalom, El Shaddiah,
He meets with me in my garden soul,
And I know He's the reason that I am made whole.
It's always so calm and His presence so strong,
So reassuring as if nothing's wrong.
And no matter how early I try to be,
He's always there *first*, just waiting on me.
Sometimes I admit that He hurts my feelings.
I don't understand His plans or His dealings.
But when the dust settles and emerges the truth
He is my Boaz, and I am His Ruth.
He is so awesome. He makes my heart shine.
I am my Beloved's and He now is mine.[1]

So that was it! My desires had not been in vain. My sweet God created that desire in me, hoping I'd choose to lavish it back on Him. What a journey I'd experienced to find the Treasure that had been beside me every step of the way. I didn't know how to explain it, but I'd never felt so loved and adored in all my life.

When I arrived at work my friend pulled me aside on the way to staff meeting. "Rebecca, what happened to you?"

My mind flipped through the last few days to figure out what she meant. I told her nothing had happened. What made her ask?

"You're face. It's glowing."

I couldn't hide the joy.

In the story of Hosea, God longed for the people of Israel to know Him as *more* than Master. So He gave Hosea the excruciating task of marrying a prostitute despite her repeated infidelity. Watching Hosea's constant love for his wife served as a living object lesson to God's people that He was their *Ish*, their Husband.

God stripped them of all they held dear and brought them into the wilderness. Not out of spite, but because He knew the wilderness would bring them to their best life— The Valley of Achor, the door of hope.

I could relate. God had removed so many things from me, it felt like I had lost it all.

And then He *benched* me.

But He benched me right next to Himself, and that was where God showed me all I would gain. He knew all along that the wilderness was best, because that's where one enters the Door of Hope. There, in the Valley of Achor, I found my Boaz, my Treasure, my *Beloved*.

May you find Him there too.

❧

WHAT I GAINED: After all the loss, my greatest gain was more of Him.

EPILOGUE

With another year of singleness under my belt, one day while walking around the trail to my park bench, I sensed something different—like maybe the dark valley was behind me. Spring danced around me, and hope began peeking out of the shadows.

I had started living again.

I'd gotten involved in a wonderful community theater, started participating in a new drama ministry at my church, and just completed the most rewarding year of teaching I'd ever experienced. I looked forward to spending the summer break in Florida with my mom.

I was finishing up a fun excursion across Texas with friends when somewhere traveling through Louisiana, my cell phone rang. My mother's voice sounded excited and emotional. She said, "Rebecca, I just gave a waitress at Bill's Diner permission to give your phone number to a wonderful

Christian man."

Bill's Diner sat just a few miles from my family home in Northeast Florida. This delicious greasy spoon wasn't fancy, but its customers boasted that it had the best comfort food this side of the St John's River. The owner, Judy, was a warm Christian woman, and she and her staff treated their regulars like family. My dad had eaten there so often, they could've changed the name to "Ivan's Diner."

I loved the place too, and anytime I came home we made it a lunch date at least once during the visit. The day of my dad's funeral, Judy and the staff opened exclusively for my family. With tenderness in their eyes, they fed us a wonderful breakfast as a way to honor my father and the friend they loved.

❧

When my mom told me what she had done, I felt as if all the color drained out of my face.

"What? Oh, Mom." Deep. Heavy. Sigh.

After last summer's painful dating experience, my heart had pulled down the shades and turned out the lights. The following months had been filled with just enough agonizing dates for me to bolt the relationship door shut.

"I don't want to go on any more dates." Besides, I didn't want to marry anyone my dad didn't know. Now that he was gone, that limited the dating selection.

That was my plan.

But God had a different one.

Judy's daughter Pam worked part-time as a waitress at the diner. After my dad died, my mom sold the house I grew up in and moved to a new part of town. Pam had gone to great lengths to find my mom's new phone number and given her a call. She said, "Mrs. Anderstrom, I can't believe I'm doing this. I promise I've never done anything like it before. I've tried to put it out of my mind, but I just can't. I'm wondering if it's the Holy Spirit compelling me to do this."

As upset as I was about my mom giving a strange man permission to call me, I admit this last phrase perked up my ears. Pam was the most reserved waitress of the group and not one to meddle into other people's lives. Given her personality, I knew it was a challenge for her to track down my mom and follow through with this call.

Pam continued, "Your husband used to come in here when Rebecca was going through such a hard time. He poured out his heart to us about her. He hurt so deeply for her."

My mom's voice quivered as she relayed Pam's words. A lump formed in my throat. I knew my dad loved me, but I never dreamed he empathized enough to share it with others.

"He told us that her spouse left her. Well, we know this man. He's a regular at the diner. He's single for the same reason, and he's just a *wonderful* Christian man. He has a little boy."

I swallowed hard.

"I was wondering if it would be okay to give him

Rebecca's number."

The next word out of my mother's mouth was, "YES."

❧

I settled into a summer routine in Florida and tried to forget the phone call about the "wonderful Christian man." Maybe if I pretended it didn't happen, it would dissipate into the Florida humidity.

It was a Thursday night. I planned to attend a Bible study at my friend's house, but then my sleepy eyelids got the best of me. I was dead asleep on the couch when the phone rang. I hate the phone and rarely answered it at my mom's, but I figured it must be my friend wondering what happened to me.

Groggy, I stumbled off the couch and grabbed the phone just as the last ring sounded. But it wasn't Lina. I heard a man's voice on the other end. "May I speak to Rebecca, please?"

My heart popped out of my chest, then looked for cover. *Oh no. It's him.*

❧

So this was *him* . . . the wonderful, Christian man. It was too late to avoid him now. Might as well get it over with. "This is she."

We talked about nothing and everything. He was intelligent, respectful, a great conversationalist, and I found myself agreeing with Pam—that he seemed to be a wonderful Christian man. An hour passed like it had only been ten minutes, and he had to hang up or he'd miss his softball game.

I made some mental notes—interesting, Christian *and* an athlete. Before we hung up, he asked if he could treat me to lunch the next day. Despite my dating ban, something about him made me want to know him. I agreed.

We went to lunch the next day. And the day after that. And the day after that. The more I got to know him, the more my heart opened up. He was different than the others. Ronnie's grounding point hung on his relationship to the Lord. He didn't depend on me or my reaction before making a decision. His life felt like true North—the same in each circumstance, regardless of who was looking or who was not.

Neither of us had any intention of dating just to date— been there, done that. Nor were we seeking a mate. My new life had gained a pleasant rhythm, and he loved his. He called me that July night out of a favor to the waitresses at Bill's Diner. If marriage was to be, then God would have to do it—which in theory is great. But the reality of vowing before God "to have and to hold from this day forth" terrified me. How would I know if this time was right? I'd thought I'd chosen correctly the last time.

As our relationship grew, so did my fears. But Ronnie continued to respond with the wisdom and strength of one who knew God. I read an article with a list of things to look for in a spouse, and he exemplified *every* one. I wondered, *what more could I want in a mate?*

One night, our conversation hinted toward marriage. Wouldn't it just be safer to stay single? Then we wouldn't run the risk of messing up again. Getting married to anyone at this stage felt like a major interruption to a perfectly good life. I asked him straight up, "Why should we get married?"

Without even taking a breath, he answered. "Because we can do more for the Lord together than we can apart."

Ding, ding, ding: good answer.

He was right. From that moment on, I knew. Two months after our first date, Ronnie asked me to marry him with his son, Chandler, by his side.

Still, the day before the wedding, my heart wouldn't stop pounding. In the middle of the preparations, I drew Ronnie aside. "I don't know if I can do this."

His face turned sober. He sat down and calmly pulled me close. "Rebecca, I love you. I want you to be my wife and the mother of our home. I have no doubt about it. But I also know this is not a simple decision for you, and if you're not ready to commit I understand. I'll be disappointed, but I'll understand." His voice was confident and true North-like, as I had come to expect.

This man.

His security in who he was apart from anyone or anything drew me to him without reserve. Whatever lay ahead, we would face it together.

The next day I said, "I do!"

⌒⌒

In my wildest dreams I couldn't have imagined what all my life would entail with Ronnie. He and Chandler have welcomed me in. We've walked through the rough and extravagant. In many ways, all those months living with the Kellys prepared me to be his wife. It taught me how to be real among people of wealth and influence. I'd need that to be Ronnie's wife. Through it all, not one experience had been wasted. Not one discovery lost.

Years earlier, I had decided I'd never know what it was like to freely love another with no fear, but I was wrong.

One day, he sent me a note. It simply said, "I love you."

The period at the end of the note had been colored in dark and was almost as large as the letters. When I asked him what that meant he said, "It means I love you. Period. Not I love you *because,* but I love you *regardless,* no matter what comes our way, no matter how you act or how you look or what you do. I'm committed to you for life. Period."

While our relationship always has room for growth, our marriage is a beautiful picture of what God meant when He created the idea. I thank Him for allowing me the privilege of being the wife to a man like Ronnie.

After years of trying to put this story of hope into words, I find myself writing this epilogue on the seventeenth anniversary weekend of our first date. After all these years, my heart swells as I smile up at God. My insides shake and I struggle to keep my composure. Not out of sadness, but out of awe at His plan.

All those months of despair, God knew what was waiting for me. Not only more of Himself, but a husband who loves the Lord—and not because anyone is checking over his shoulder, but because it's who he is from the inside out.

I wouldn't trade my time on the bench next to Him for anything. The gain of Him far outweighs the loss. That was gift enough. But as He is prone to do when He chooses to shower us with blessings, God had *extra* whipped cream and a cherry on top waiting for me—a God-fearing man, Ronnie Fussell, and his darling son, Chandler.

Oh, what I gained when I lost it all.

ACKNOWLEDGMENTS

In the early days when writing a book was more of a passing fancy than a you-can't-die-until-you-finish-it project, after reading other author's acknowledgment pages, I learned something very quickly: no one writes a book alone. I marveled at the people who cheered for and encouraged the various authors, and I wondered where I could find people like that.

I prayed for help. And oh boy, did God send it. Each one of the individuals mentioned here has played a unique role, and I can't imagine my life or this project without them.

To my grandmother Dorothy, who never wrote a book—just a community newsletter for her age-restricted mobile-home park—but her sentences splashed and danced off the page like Gene Kelly in *Singing in the Rain*. Who knew words could make the world of shuffleboard and giant tricycles so captivating. Her articles sparked my imagination and tickled my funny bone. Thank you for being you and spilling over on to me.

To my brother Rodney and my friend Heather, who get the brave-heart award for graciously accepting my invitation to read my first (and very awful I might add) draft. You were a safe place for my wobbly story to try its wings. May your reward be deep for that excruciating labor of love.

To my editors Leslie, Shalyn and Top whose expertise and insight helped unearth the truths buried behind all the words. Your gift is unsung, but so very vital. Thank you for your patience with me.

To my book club buddies Christy, Connie, Karen, Lisa, Meloni, Patricia and Robin who have stood behind and beside me on this journey. Hashing out life with you keeps me sane—for the most part. HA! You are my forever friends. We have too many pinky-swears not to be. I treasure Saturday mornings with you.

To my bestie Robin Lynette, bless you for securing my secrets in your vault, and for promising to bury my journals when I die. Thank you for clapping for me and acting like I was a real author or something. You're the real author. You just don't realize that yet. When I grow up, I want to be like you.

To my prayer partner Lora, who year after year continued praying and lifting up this book as if God would really use it. Your life is a living example of bearing one another's burdens. You are a friend through laughter and pain. I love our Sunday lunches and going to the Throne with you.

To my cheerleader Stephanie, who refused to believe that writing this book was just a whim. Thank you for pushing me and asking tough questions. God always sent you at *precisely* the right time.

To my Sequel Sisters Christine, Ellen, Erin, Jeanne, Lea Ann, Nina, Robin and Ruth. Who knew when we met at Mary's Intensive we'd be friends for life? You are like oxygen to my soul. You have carried my burdens and shared in my joys. You are safe. You show me Jesus. You "one-another" me in ways I've only dreamed of. What a treasure. What a find! I thank God for bringing us together, and I relish our times together. Thank you, Marco Polo.

Special thanks to my dear friend Christine for the time invested reading these words and the deep insights shared to make them better. Your spontaneous prayers take me to the Father's Throne, and your perspectives are heart changing. If I could see the Holy Spirit, I think He would look an awful lot like you.

To my writers' critique group, Joe, Lou Ann, Lynn, Nike and Tracy, who handle each critique with the gentle firmness of one polishing antique silver. Your spirit of grace and truth blows through our space, leaving me refreshed and rejuvenated in ways I haven't experienced in ages. Time with you reminds me of who God made me to be, and it's so thrilling I can't sleep when I leave.

To my siblings, Ross, Rhonda, Reed and Rodney, I love being one of the five Rs. You make me proud to be a part of the Anderstrom tribe. I thank God for blending our family together. I love you and all your mates and kids too.

To my mom and my biggest supporter, who would buy this book for the whole world if she could. Thank you for loving me and encouraging me to try. I thank God He allowed me to belong to you. I love you.

To Chandler, who graciously accepted me with very little notice. I love you. You welcomed me into you and your dad's world, and I could never thank you enough for that. You are a true gentleman and pure delight to your dad and me.

To my sweet husband, Ronnie, who has never made fun of me for the gazillion hours I've spent on this project but has only supported and cheered me on. Thank you for letting me dream and follow the paths God designed for me. I *love* being one with you!

And to my first reader, Jesus, who has read every word—the ones printed and the ones tucked away for His eyes alone. You are my Boaz. I wouldn't want to live one *second* without you. I love you too.

END NOTES

Endorsements
1. John Forgerty, "Put Me in, Coach" (Warner Bros. Records) 1985.

Introduction
1. Bella DePaulo Ph.D., What is the divorce rate really? https://www.psychologytoday.com/us/blog/living-single/201702/what-is-the-divorce-rate-really.

Chapter 2:
1. A.W. Tozer, *The Pursuit of God* (Columbia, SC: Millennium Publications, 2014), 15.

Chapter 3:
1. II Corinthians 12:9.
2. Shannan Martin, *Falling Free* (Nashville, TN: Thomas Nelson, 2016), 110.

Chapter 4:
1. Ann Voskamp, *One Thousand Gifts* (Grand Rapids, MI: Zondervan, 2010), 135.

Chapter 5:
1. Ecclesiastes 3: 3-6.

Chapter 6:
1. Matthew 7:11(ESV).

Chapter 9:
1. Emily P. Freeman, *Grace for the Good Girl* (Grand Rapids, MI: Revell, 2011), 24.

Chapter: 10
1. Dr. Henry Cloud, Dr. John Townsend, *Safe People* (Grand Rapids, MI: Zondervan, 1995), 97.
2. Romans 8:28.
3. Ephesians 4:25.

4. Romans 12:19.
5. II Chronicles 16:9.

Chapter 11:
1. Deuteronomy 33:27.

Chapter 12:
1. Gerald Sittser, *A Grace Disguised* (Grand Rapids, MI: Zondervan, 1995), 52.
2. II Corinthians 10: 4-5.
3. Katie Davis Majors, *Daring to Hope* (Colorado Springs: Multnomah, 2017), 34.
4. Gerald Sittser, *A Grace Disguised* (Grand Rapids, MI: Zondervan, 1995), 137.

Chapter 13:
1. Gerry Sittser, *A Grace Disguised*, (Grand Rapids, MI: Zondervan, 1995), 70.
2. Matthew 18:21-22.
3. Psalm 103:14.
4. Psalm 62:8.

Chapter 14:
1. Katharina A. von Schlegel, *Be Still My Soul,* Public Domain, 1752.

Chapter 15:
1. Deuteronomy 33:27.

Chapter 16:
1. C.S Lewis, A Grief Observed, (New York: Bantam, 1961), 54.

Chapter 17:
1. Romans 8:28.
2. Luke 10:41 & 42.
3. Sara Haggerty, *Every Bitter Thing is Sweet*, (Grand Rapids, MI: Zondervan, 2014), 179.
4. Beth Moore, *Audacious*, (Nashville, TN: B&H Publishing Group, 2015), 84.

Chapter 21:
1. This last thought is taken from Song of Solomon 7:10

REBECCA LYNN FUSSELL loves her God, her family, her friends, TAB & Chocolate . . . ok, yeah, and Herschel Walker, the wonder dog. (Yes! They are big Georgia Bulldog fans.) She loves creating something out of nothing, but her greatest delight is sharing the freeing truth of God's word and watching people become who God meant for them to be. She adores the arts and believes God can use it to reach and minister to people in unique and powerful ways. *Maybe one day she'll get to own her own art house!*

She's been an insulin dependent diabetic for over 39 years, and she's still learning how to manage it all. And something she never dreamed she would be saying, but it's true. Rebecca has no children of her own. Her husband Ronnie does have a darling son, Chandler, who she loves and enjoys very much.

Her days are filled with writing (and editing!), learning, teaching, reading and definitely staying in touch with friends! Oh, and washing a few loads of laundry and making a meal or two and cleaning up the house and . . . well, you get the picture.

Rebecca has created a *special playlist* for each chapter of BENCHED. Find it at **rebeccafussell.com**